Norwegians

IN MINNESOTA

Jon Gjerde and Carlton C. Qualey

Foreword by Bill Holm

Published in cooperation with the
Norwegian-American Historical Association

MINNESOTA HISTORICAL SOCIETY PRESS

Publication of this book was supported, in part, with funds provided by the June D. Holmquist Publication Endowment Fund of the Minnesota Historical Society.

www.mnhs.org/mhspress

Manufactured in Canada

10 9 8 7 6 5 4 3 2 1

International Standard Book Number: 0-87351-421-1

♾ The paper used in this publication meets the minimum requirements of the American National Standard for Information Sciences Permanence for Printed Library Materials, ANSI Z39.48-1984.

Library of Congress Cataloging-in-Publication Data

Gjerde, Jon, 1953–
   Norwegians in Minnesota / Jon Gjerde and Carlton C. Qualey ; foreword by Bill Holm.
     p.   cm. — (The people of Minnesota)
   Includes bibliographical references and index.
   ISBN 0-87351-421-1 (pbk. : alk. paper)
     1. Norwegian Americans—Minnesota—History. 2. Minnesota—History.
   3. Minnesota—Ethnic relations. I. Qualey, Carlton C. (Carlton Chester), 1904–
   II. Title. III. Series.

F615.S2 Q35 2002
977.6'0043982—dc21

                                2002016515

This book was designed and set in type by Wendy Holdman, Stanton Publication Services, Saint Paul, Minnesota; and was printed by Friesens, Altona, Manitoba.

Contents

Foreword

by Bill Holm

Human beings have not been clever students at learning any lessons from their three or four thousand odd years of recorded history. We repeat our mistakes from generation to generation with tedious regularity. But we ought to have learned at least one simple truth: that there is no word, no idea that is not a double-edged sword. Take, for example, the adjective *ethnic*. In one direction, it cuts upward, to show us the faces, the lives, the histories of our neighbors and ourselves. It shows us that we are not alone on this planet—that we are all rooted with deep tendrils growing down to our ancestors and the stories of how they came to be not *there*, but *here*. These tendrils are visible in our noses and cheekbones, our middle-aged diseases and discomforts, our food, our religious habits, our celebrations, our manner of grieving, our very names. The fact that here in Minnesota, at any rate, we mostly live together in civil harmony—showing sometimes affectionate curiosity, sometimes puzzled irritation but seldom murderous violence—speaks well for our progress as a community of neighbors, even as members of a civilized human tribe.

But early in this new century in America we have seen the dark blade of the ethnic sword made visible, and it has cut us to the quick. From at least one angle, our national wounds from terrorist attacks are an example of ethnicity gone mad, tribal loyalty whipped to fanatical hysteria, until it turns human beings into monstrous machines of mass murder. Few tribes own a guiltless history in this regard.

The 20th century did not see much progress toward solving the problem of ethnicity. Think of Turk and Armenian, German and Jew, Hutu and Tutsi, Protestant and Catholic, Albanian and Serb, French and Algerian—think of our own lynchings. We all hoped for better from the 21st century but may not get any reprieve at all from the tidal waves of violence and hatred.

As global capitalism breaks down the borders between nation-states, fanatical ethnicity rises to life like a hydra. Cheerful advertisements assure us that we are all a family—wearing the same pants, drinking the same pop, singing and going on line together as we spend. When we invoke *family,* we don't seen to remember well the ancient Greek family tragedies. We need to make not a family but a civil community of neighbors, who may neither spend nor look alike but share a desire for truthful history—an alert curiosity about the stories and the lives of our neighbors and a respect both for difference—and for privacy. We must get the metaphors right; we are neither brothers nor sisters here in Minnesota, nor even cousins. We are neighbors, all us *ethnics,* and that fact imposes on us a stricter obligation than blood and, to the degree to which we live up to it, makes us civilized.

As both Minnesotans and Americans, none of us can escape the fact that we *ethnics,* in historic terms, have hardly settled here for the length of a sneeze. Most of us have barely had time to lose the language of our ancestors or to produce protein-stuffed children half a foot taller than ourselves. What does a mere century or a little better amount to in history? Even the oldest settlers—the almost ur-inhabitants, the Dakota and Ojibwa—emigrated here from elsewhere on the continent. The Jeffers Petroglyphs in southwest Minnesota are probably the oldest evidence we have of any human habitation. They are still and will most likely remain only shadowy tellers of any historic truth about us. Who made this language? History is silent. The only clear facts scholars agree on about these mysterious pictures carved in hard red Sioux quartzite is that they were the work of neither of the current native tribes and can be scientifically dated only between the melting of the last glacier and the arrival of the first European settlers in the territory. They seem very old to the eye. It is good for us, I think, that our history begins not with certainty, but with mystery, cause for wonder rather than warfare.

In 1978, before the first edition of this ethnic survey appeared, a researcher came to Minneota to interview local people for information about the Icelanders. Tiny though their numbers, the Icelanders were a real ethnic group with their own language, history, and habits of mind. They settled in the late 19th century in three small clumps around Minneota. At that time, I could still introduce this researcher to a few old ladies born in Iceland and to a dozen children of immigrants who grew up with English as a second language, thus with thick accents. The old still prayed the Lord's Prayer in Icelandic, to them the language of Jesus himself, and a handful of people could still read the ancient poems and sagas in the leather-covered editions brought as treasures from the old country. But two decades have wiped out that primary source. The first generation is gone, only a few alert and alive in the second, and the third speaks only English—real Americans in hardly a century. What driblets of Icelandic blood remain are mixed with a little of this, a little of that. The old thorny names, so difficult to pronounce, have been respelled, then corrected for sound.

Is this the end of ethnicity? The complete meltdown into history evaporated into global marketing anonymity? I say no. On a late October day, a letter arrives from a housewife in Nevis, Minnesota. She's never met me, but she's been to Iceland now and met unknown cousins she found on an Internet genealogy search. The didactic voice in my books reminds her of her father's voice: "He could've said that. Are we *all* literary?" We've never met, she confesses, but she gives me enough of her family tree to convince me that we might be cousins fifteen generations back. She is descended, she says with pride, from the Icelandic law speaker in 1063, Gunnar the Wise. She knows now that she is not alone in history. She has shadowing names, even dates, in her very cells. She says—with more smug pride—that her vinarterta (an Icelandic immigrant prune cake that is often the last surviving ghost of the old country) is better than any she ate in Iceland. She invites me to sample a piece if I ever get to Nevis. Who says there is no profit and joy in ethnicity? That killjoy has obviously never tasted vinarterta!

I think what is happening in this letter, both psychologically and culturally, happens simultaneously in the lives of hundreds of thousands of Minnesotans and countless millions of Americans. Only the details differ, pilaf, jiaozi, fry bread, collards, latkes, or menudo rather than vinarterta, but the process and the object remain the same. We came to this cold flat place so far from the sea in wave after wave of immigration—filling up the steadily fewer empty places in this vast midsection of a continent—but for all of us, whatever the reason for our arrival: poverty, political upheaval, ambition—we check most of our history, and thus our inner life, at the door of the new world. For a while, old habits and even the language carry on, but by the third generation, history is lost. Yet America's history, much less Minnesota's, is so tiny, so new, so uncertain, so much composed of broken connections—and now of vapid media marketing—that we feel a loneliness for a history that stretches back further into the life of the planet. We want more cousins so that, in the best sense, we can be better neighbors. We can acquire interior weight that will keep us rooted in our new homes. That is why we need to read these essays on the ethnic history of Minnesota. We need to meet those neighbors and listen to new stories.

We need also the concrete underpinning of facts that they provide to give real body to our tribal myths if those myths are not to drift off into nostalgic vapor. Svenskarnas Dag and Santa Lucia Day will not tell us much about the old Sweden that disgorged so many of its poor to Minnesota. At the height of the Vietnam War, an old schoolmate of mine steeled his courage to confess to his stern Swedish father that he was thinking both of conscientious objection and, if that didn't work, escape to Canada. He expected patriotic disdain, even contempt. Instead the upright old man wept and cried, "So soon again!" He had left Sweden early in the century to avoid the compulsory military draft but told that history to none of his children. The history of our arrival here does not lose its nobility by being filled with draft-dodging, tubercular lungs, head lice, poverty, failure. It gains humanity. We are all members of a very big club—and not an exclusive one.

I grew up in western Minnesota surrounded by accents: Icelandic, Norwegian, Swedish, Belgian, Dutch, German, Polish, French Canadian, Irish, even a Yankee or two, a French Jewish doctor, and a Japanese chicken sexer in Dr. Kerr's chicken hatchery. As a boy, I thought that a fair-sized family of nations. Some of those tribes have declined almost to extinction, and new immigrants have come to replace them: Mexican, Somali, Hmong, and Balkan. Relations are sometimes awkward as the old ethnicities bump their aging dispositions against the new, forgetting that their own grandparents spoke English strangely, dressed in odd clothes, and ate foods that astonished and sometimes repulsed their neighbors. History does not cease moving at the exact moment we begin to occupy it comfortably.

I've taught many Laotian students in my freshman English classes at Southwest State University in Marshall. I always assign papers on family history. For many children of the fourth generation, the real stories have evaporated, but for the Hmong, they are very much alive—escape followed by gunfire, swimming the Mekong, a childhood in Thai refugee camps. One student brought a piece of his mother's intricate embroidery to class and translated its symbolic storytelling language for his classmates. Those native-born children of farmers will now be haunted for life by the dark water of the Mekong. Ethnic history is alive and surprisingly well in Minnesota.

Meanwhile the passion for connection—thus a craving for a deeper history—has blossomed grandly in my generation and the new one in front of it. A Canadian professional genealogist at work at an immigrant genealogical center at Hofsos in north Iceland assures me, as fact, that genealogy has surpassed, in raw numbers, both stamp and coin collecting as a hobby. What will it next overtake? Baseball cards? Rock and roll 45 rpms? It's a sport with a future, and these essays on ethnic history are part of the evidence of its success.

I've even bought a little house in Hofsos, thirty miles south of the Arctic Circle where in the endless summer light I watch loads of immigrant descendants from Canada and the United States arrive clutching old brown-tone photos, yellowed letters in languages they don't read, the misspelled name of Grandpa's farm. They feed their information into computers and comb through heavy books, hoping to find the history lost when their ancestors simplified their names at Ellis Island or in Quebec. To be ethnic, somehow, is to be human. Neither can we escape it, nor should we want to. You cannot interest yourself in the lives of your neighbors if you don't take sufficient interest in your own.

Minnesotans often jokingly describe their ethnic backgrounds as "mongrel"—a little of this, a little of that, who knows what? But what a gift to be a mongrel! So many ethnicities and so little time in life to track them down! You will have to read many of these essays to find out who was up to what, when. We should also note that every one of us on this planet is a mongrel, thank God. The mongrel is the strongest and longest lived of dogs—and of humans, too. Only the dead are pure—and then, only in memory, never in fact. Mongrels do not kill each other to maintain the pure ideology of the tribe. They just go on mating, acquiring a richer ethnic history with every passing generation. So I commend this series to you. Let me introduce you to your neighbors. May you find pleasure and wisdom in their company.

Norwegians

IN MINNESOTA

Ruth Elenor Lerud, a 4-H club member who grew up on a farm near Twin Valley, won a trip to the Minnesota State Fair in 1935 as bread-baking champion of Norman County. All four of her grandparents were Norwegian immigrants, and she grew up speaking only Norwegian before she began school. The community of her childhood was so thoroughly Norwegian that ethnicity was rarely a topic of conversation. Her grandparents never learned English, and her parents spoke Norwegian with them and at community events such as threshing bees, potato picking, and silo filling.

A N ELDERLY NORWEGIAN AMERICAN living in Minneapolis in the 1950s pointed proudly to the fact that "no State in the Union and no American city of the first class have proportionately as many people of Norwegian blood. I was impressed by this back in the old homeland. . . . Even the school children . . . would talk about all those people going to America. Indelibly implanted in my mind even now is a remark made by one of my school mates . . . 'And they are all bound for Minnesota.' "[1]

Although the schoolmate exaggerated a bit, Minnesota attracted more of the approximately 850,000 Norwegians who immigrated between 1825 and 1928 than any other state. It became both a population and a cultural center for Norwegian Americans, and they became its third largest ethnic group. Norwegians began to arrive in the United States in large numbers in the late 1840s, rising in 1882 to 28,500 persons. The number of Norwegians born in Minnesota peaked in 1905 with 111,611; five years later the census counted 105,302, more than 26% of those in the entire United States and more than the next two leading states of Wisconsin and North Dakota combined. The Norwegian American community in Minnesota has not only persisted, it has flourished. In 1970, 156,841 Minnesotans claimed Norwegian as their mother tongue. In the subsequent censuses when Minnesotans were asked to name their ancestries, the numbers were even greater. In 1990, some 757,212 Minnesota residents identified themselves as being of Norwegian ancestry, a population that equals over 17% of the state's population or, put differently, is more than the combined inhabitants of Ramsey and St. Louis Counties. Minnesota outstrips all other states in Norwegian identification by a huge margin. The state nearest Minnesota's total is Wisconsin with 416,271 residents. One might go even further to say that even those Minnesotans who do not

Proud descendants of Norwegian immigrants who arrived on the sloop *Restauration* in 1825 posed with a model of the wooden ship at the centennial celebration of Norwegian immigration to the U.S. at the Minnesota State Fairgrounds in 1925.

claim a Norwegian heritage live in a state indelibly identified with Norway. It is no coincidence that one of the state's most prevalent late 20th-century symbols is the Viking or that the Norwegian bachelor farmer is a stock image of Minnesota life.[2]

Why did Norwegians emigrate in such large numbers to Minnesota? Part of the answer is simply that the Norwegian emigration was huge. In the 19th century only the famine-stricken Irish exceeded the emigration rate of the Norwegians. Like other European nations in the mid-19th century, Norway experienced wrenching economic changes and a doubling of its population from 1815 to 1865. The latter resulted primarily from a declining infant and child mortality rate. Per capita agriculture output rose 70% from 1800 to 1830, but the country was, and is, both mountainous and forested, with little arable land. Job opportunities in its agricultural, fishing, and lumbering economy were limited. Many young people were forced to seek day-laboring jobs on the farms of others, while a second, more diverse group called *husmenn* (cotters), whose rights and duties varied by region, formed a kind of intermediate rural class between the independent farm owners who were called *bønder*, and the day laborers. More intensive cultivation and the colonization of northern Norway supported a 27% increase in the *bønder* between 1801 and 1855. But at the same time the number of *husmenn* nearly doubled and day laborers trebled."[3]

No massive emigration resulted, however, until the mid-1860s when a combination of overpopulation, food shortages, mechanization, and changing market structures led to farm foreclosures. Even worse, poor crops, coupled with the disappearance of the fickle spring herring run from the Norwegian coasts, resulted in actual starvation. Infant mortality rose, and there were reports of bread made from tree bark. The country's belated experience with mechanization worked to increase emigration. Between 1865 and 1900 the agricultural labor force was reduced by some 50,000, and the number of *husmenn* fell by half to less than 25,000 as many of them swelled the stream of emigrants. With the decline in the availability of cheap labor, farm owners began to invest in harvesting and sowing machines, potato diggers, and selfbinders. Higher wages, increased production per man hour, and improved transportation would militate against further starving times, but many small *bønder* could not afford to mechanize and were forced to sell out. With the displaced farm laborers and cotters, they found their way to the slowly industrializing Norwegian cities. Information about America and the rich farmlands of its Midwest, however, opened another, more attractive option to these people and led them to consider emigrating. Land in Minnesota became available to white settlers just as Norwegians forsook their homeland.[4]

The rapid changes in Norwegian society were accompanied by a pietistic religious movement, inspired by the late 18th-century leadership of Hans Nielsen Hauge, and by a blossoming of romantic nationalism. The latter regarded rural society as truly Norwegian, while viewing the urban community as hopelessly compromised by its ties to Denmark and Sweden, which had successively ruled Norway for four centuries. The two movements introduced new ideas and contributed to the creation of an increasingly assertive and nationalistic peasant class (*bonde*), resentful of the pretensions of the official and clerical classes, distrustful of Danish language and customs, and dedicated to perpetuating Norwegian rural life and culture.[5]

Ironically, it may have been the conservatism of the Norwegian farmers that in part prompted them to make the radical decision to move to the New World rather than to Norway's cities, as Norwegian historian Ingrid Semmingsen contended. By emigrating, they believed their rural way of life could be maintained without the overpopulation and socioeconomic problems existing at home. Although their motivation to migrate was primarily economic in nature, the rural Norwegians' desire to perpetuate rural life and their distrust of the city provided a cultural background important in the development of the 19th- and early 20th-century Norwegian American community. In Minnesota, Norwegians took land in rural areas, where they clung to traditions and patterns that provided some continuity with the homeland.[6] The parish church, for example, remained the central institution, and the rural immigrants, some of whom had been active participants in Norway's social reforms, quickly became involved in the Minnesota political scene.

Settlement Patterns

The earliest emigrants left Norway in 1825, settling ultimately in Illinois after a stay in New York. By the late 1830s Norwegians were to be found in the Wisconsin areas that would become mother settlements for the first influx to Minnesota in the 1850s. The best known of the southeastern Wisconsin concentrations were located at Muskego

A historic building of national significance for Norwegian Americans is the Muskego Church, a log meeting house that was the first Norwegian Lutheran church built in the U.S. Constructed in 1843–44 near Muskego, Wisconsin, near Milwaukee, the church was moved to the campus of Luther Seminary in St. Paul in 1904.

in Waukesha County; Jefferson and Rock Prairie in Rock County; Koshkonong in Dane, Jefferson, and Rock Counties; and Wiola, Spring Prairie, and Bonnet Prairie in Lafayette and Columbia Counties.

These early immigrants had been the victims of "America fever," which reached epidemic proportions in the 1860s. Its spread throughout the mountains and valleys of Norway was fanned by the so-called America letters written by friends and relatives who had gone to the United States. Though some were negative in their accounts of the everyday conditions of American life, many enthusiastically described the abundance of land, the higher wages, and other wonders. Handed from neighbor to neighbor and from parish to parish, a single letter might be read and copied hundreds of times.[7]

Areas of Norwegian Settlement in Minnesota

One example of these influential missives will perhaps suggest something of their fervor and flavor. Jens Grønbek wrote from Rice County, Minnesota, to his brother-in-law, Christian Heltzen of Hemnes in Nordland, Norway, in September 1867: "You ask that I report to you concerning conditions here. . . . America is a naturally rich land, endowed with virtually everything, except to a dull-witted European who is disappointed not to find money in the streets or who expects to get things without moving his arms. . . .

"There are many thousand acres of available land here — government, school, and railroad land — although it is increasingly in the West. As for government or homestead land, one can take a quarter section or 160 acres free, except for payment of a registration fee of $14 per quarter, and this is almost all arable land. . . .

"Do you know what, my dear Christian? If you find farming in Norway unrewarding and your earnings at sea are poor, I advise you, as your friend and brother-in-law, to abandon everything, and — if you can raise $600 — to come to Minnesota. Do not believe that all is lies and fables in reports that in one year in America all will be well, for I can testify that it is true, despite the fact that, last fall when I came, I thought for a time I would starve. But an American came to me in friendly fashion and said, "Huad yuh want? Want yuh work? Will yuh have som ting to eat and trink?" That is, did I need anything, did I want work, and was I hungry? I did not understand him and continued hungry even though I had been offered all these good things.

"I have now worked for a Norwegian farmer since Christmas and will remain here until October. I have it very good here. Five meals each day of the best food in the world, so that I fear I have become choosy. . . .

"Now, dear Christian, if you consider selling and emigrating across the Atlantic Ocean, please write me. Do not be worried about the voyage, either for your wife or for the children. Neither should you be alarmed about Indians or other trolls in America, for the former are now chased away, and the Yankees, that is Americans, are as kind a folk toward a stranger as I can imagine."

". . . I have met no acquaintances from Norway since Christmas. Nearly all newcomers want to return to the homeland until they have become American citizens, and then hardly anyone wants to return."

Such letters not only determined patterns of emigration from the homeland, they also influenced Norwegian patterns of settlement in the United States. Those who emigrated wrote back to their home regions, and others then decided to follow. The Stavanger district on the west coast of Norway was an area of early emigration. America fever then moved north up the coast and into the mountains to the east. Well into the 1860s most emigrants left Norway's inner fjords and high mountain districts, but the whole nation was stricken at one time or another.[8]

Once in the United States, the immigrant often made his or her way to a settlement from which letters had been sent. In the beginning this process produced homogeneous rural communities in which only certain districts or parishes in Norway were represented. "A remarkable aspect of the tendency of the Norwegian immigrants to flock together was that it was not enough for them to seek out fellow Norwegians," wrote Theodore C. Blegen. "They went further and associated themselves with people who had come from the very valley" they had left. As settlement continued, the groups became more heterogeneous, retaining, however, a common base of Norwegianness.

In the 1850s the attention of Norwegian immigrants focused on Minnesota Territory. The first permanent Norwegian colonies were begun by groups of settlers who migrated from Wisconsin to the oak-opening lands along the Mississippi River in southeastern Minnesota. By 1880 numerous settlements dotted a block of counties—Houston, Fillmore, Goodhue, Freeborn, Mower, Dodge, part of Olmsted, Rice, Faribault, Steele, and Waseca—which became the first major concentration of Norwegians in Minnesota.[9]

The peopling of this area and other parts of the state where farming was the main occupation resulted from a three-stage chain migration, a process that was repeated many times as the immigrants moved westward. In the first stage, families sailed from Norway to form a new settlement in, say, Wisconsin. From their new homes they wrote back to friends and relatives in their old parishes, encouraging others to join them. With high birth rates and the arrival of more and more people, the first-stage settlement area soon became too crowded. Newcomers then stayed only a short time before moving on to cheaper lands farther west—thus creating a second settlement.

The third stage in the migration pattern came into being as others were drawn to the second settlement directly from Norway by the need for workers on the frontier. Minnesota farmers received laborers they could trust by sending prepaid tickets to friends and relatives in Norway. Of the emigrants leaving Christiania (now Oslo) between 1872 and 1875, for example, 39% had received prepaid tickets.[10]

Spring Grove Township in Houston County, an area within the first Minnesota concentration, illustrates this migration process and its lingering effects. Beginning in 1852, when it received some of "the first half-dozen permanent Norwegian settlers in all of Minnesota," Spring Grove Township went on to become "one of the most densely settled Norwegian American colonies in the United States" and "one of the important distribution points for Norwegian settlement in the American Northwest." In 1870 Spring Grove had a total of 1,135 Norwegians and only a few dozen others. Many of its early settlers were born in Hallingdal, and they had spent some time in Rock County, Wisconsin, before moving to Minnesota in 1852. Plat maps of the area show that these Hallings tended to settle together in the township, where they were joined by immigrants

Members of the Rosendahl family and others posed with a Norwegian-style hayrack called a *kubberulle* on the Paul and Gunhild Rosendahl farm near Spring Grove about 1900. Cartoonist (and photographer) Peter Rosendahl took the picture. It's fairly late to be using a pioneer-era old-country wagon like this one, but the Rosendahls had the skills to make one.

who arrived directly from Hallingdal as well as from various other regions.[11]

In spite of the fact that people from throughout Norway could eventually be found in Spring Grove, it retained traces of the Halling subculture into the 1930s. For three to four generations the language lingered, along with some old Norwegian agricultural customs. Farms "among the trees were built little by little" until there was "a cluster of small buildings consisting of horse stable, cow barn, sheepfold, hog barn, doghouse, chicken house, wagon shed, granary, corncrib, hay sheds—merely a roof supported by four posts—even a smokehouse for meats, [and a] privy, in addition to the residence, which was the first erected. All of these were built and arranged somewhat like farm places in Norway." The grouping of friends and relatives from Hallingdal also made it easier to maintain the regional dialect. One resident in 1920 recalled a Halling "who left some fine talented boys who neither despise their

The solidly Norwegian town of Spring Grove welcomed the Hallinglag *stevne*, as annual *bygdelag* gatherings were called, with banners and Norwegian and American flags in June 1912. The Chris Engell & Son studio photographed many of the town's ethnic events.

mother tongue nor are ashamed of being of Norwegian descent. Furthermore one of them can both write and speak such genuine Halling dialect that it is as if he were raised in Hallingdal itself."

But the most visible manifestation of the bridges between the Norwegian and Norwegian American cultures in Spring Grove and in Norwegian America as a whole was the Lutheran church. Still dotting the rural Minnesota landscape, their white spires once marked the social and religious centers of the rural communities. In Spring Grove the building of a church was preceded by the formation of a congregation in 1855 in a settler's home. Because of the chain migration pattern, congregations were usually formed by a group from a certain district in the homeland. The call to a pastor then went out, but because of the scarcity of ordained ministers, especially in the early years, several fledgling parishes were often served by a single Lutheran pastor. The thirst for his services is illustrated by the mission of one pioneer minister who visited a pastorless area of southeastern Minnesota in 1857. While there, he celebrated communion for 60 persons, churched 21 women after childbirth, christened 21 children, catechized eight and confirmed six youths, and performed services— all in the course of one day and two "wakeful nights."

Following the call to a minister, the congregation then set about the construction of a church and a parsonage. In Spring Grove the Norwegians erected a stone church in 1860, which was served by a minister who had emigrated directly from Norway three years before. Members contributed sizable sums for these structures, which were frequently built when money was scarce. At such times, the people resorted to another custom common in Norway— the payment of tithes in agricultural produce.[12]

Taaran Vik and her pupils gathered outside the Norwegian parochial school near Echo, Yellow Medicine County, in 1915. Rock Valle Lutheran Church members sponsored the school.

Once built, the church quickly became the heart of the community. As one observer put it, "If one did not come to worship God, one might come for other purposes, such as trading horses, assigning road work, hiring thrashers, or hearing the latest news." Another immigrant recalled that the churchgoers often gathered from long distances. "They usually walked. They left early and might stand outside the

church to wait for each other. They were so happy to meet and find out if everything was well, and then they were so eager to find out if anyone had received a letter from Norway, because almost all of them longed to hear news from the home *bygd* [district or rural community]."[13]

Another factor that influenced Norwegian patterns of settlement as well as the retention of Norwegian rural cultural traits in the United States was the immigration of families. In the 1850s, 32% of all Norwegian emigrants were children under 12 years of age. The ratio of males to females was at first unusually equal. In Spring Grove, for example, the 1870 sex ratio was 107.9 males for each 100 females, a far more balanced proportion than the 127.7 males per 100 females in the state as a whole. Many of the community's children had been born in Norway, and there were 628 young people under 19 as opposed to only 403 persons between 20 and 49.[14]

Given this preponderance of young people, it was not surprising that as the southeastern Minnesota communities grew older, overpopulation again acted as a push factor in the further migrations of young Norwegian Americans. In fact, many children of Norwegian immigrants experienced a period of crisis when they came of age because of their many siblings. Often they were unable to wed because of the paucity of resources upon which to base a marriage. Research has indicated that in some rural settlements the rates of marriage were lower than in Norway. The Norwegian bachelor farmer has a long historical profile. As had been the case in Norway, some were able to take over the family farms, but many were forced to move to the cities or to less crowded lands farther west. The westward movement thus was a combination of people seeking their fortunes and others forced off their home farm. "The America fever has raged in many places in old Norway," wrote a clergyman in 1885, who was cognizant of the perception of opportunity to the west. "This fever is not always quieted by the establishment of a home in the New World. Those who live in the older settlements learn that great reaches of fertile and free lands are to be had to the westward, and so they again turn toward the new and the unseen."[15]

Some migrated to the so-called Linden settlement to the west in Blue Earth, Brown, and Watonwan Counties, an area unique among pre-Civil War Norwegian settlements in Minnesota because it was located on the prairie. After 1865 many more chose the Park Region of west-central Minnesota, the second major Norwegian concentration in the state. Bordered on the west by the Red River Valley and on the northeast by pine forests, this rolling, well-watered, wooded region contained 6,175 Norwegians in 1870 and 15,859 in 1875—25% of its total population. By 1909 it featured "an almost unbroken series of Norwegian settlements" and not less than 100,000 Norwegians. One man wrote that nearly all of its thousands of lakes were surrounded by their homes.[16]

Many of these later settlements in western and central

The Park Region Ski Club attracted skiers from as far away as Chicago and a crowd of more than 3,000 to its snowy 1913 meet in Fergus Falls, where professionals and amateurs competed separately. The contestant climbing the ski jump in the background may have made that year's longest jump, 120 feet, to claim a prize of $40.00.

The small community of Sogn in Goodhue County shows what rural life was like for Norwegian farmers in southeastern Minnesota on a busy summer day about 1910. The Sogn Valley has preserved its rural ethnic identity so well that a part of it near the hamlet pictured here, the Nansen Agricultural Historic District, was designated in 2000 the first agricultural historic district in the state of Minnesota.

Minnesota were offshoots of those in the southeast. Just as land in Goodhue County had been taken up by Norwegians from Wisconsin, so were portions of Lac qui Parle County, in the upper Minnesota River Valley, the "daughters" of Goodhue. In the 1870s a "considerable migration" occurred when "no more land was available in Goodhue," wrote Olaf O. Stageberg. Many migrants then went to Lac qui Parle, so that "anyone who travels around in these two counties, as I have done, finds the same names in both places." As had been the case with the earlier Wisconsin colonies, the southeastern Minnesota areas became mother settlements, serving as jumping-off places for new emigrants from Norway. The first-stage Valdris settlement in Holden and Warsaw Townships of Goodhue County, for example, "served for a long time as the destination" of numerous Norwegians who emigrated from the Valdris region in Norway. As the Goodhue County area filled up, the three-stage process was repeated. Most latecomers remained "there only a short while," wrote O. J. Flaten, before going farther west where open land was still available and where second-stage Valdris settlements were then created.[17]

The Spring Grove Norwegians also participated in this

process. In 1865 six families that had originally emigrated from two parishes in Hallingdal moved from Spring Grove to a second-stage settlement that became known as Big Grove near Brooten in southwestern Stearns County. Others from Spring Grove and from Hallingdal followed, with Spring Grove acting as a mother settlement for Hallings who stopped there for a time before pushing farther west.

The neatly fenced farmstead of Ole and Helina Halvorson family near Brooten in Stearns County, around 1910. North Dakota photographer John Johnson made the rounds of Norwegian farms in southwestern Stearns County during 1910, taking photos of families and their farms.

Hallings made up nearly 70% of the foreign-born members of the Big Grove Norwegian Lutheran Church. Some 10% hailed from mountainous Telemark, whose earliest representatives had reached Spring Grove from Winnebago County, Wisconsin, about the same time as the Rock County Hallings, and about 20% had been born in other parts of Norway.[18]

The latter were frequently lured to the new settlements by notices in Norwegian-language newspapers praising their prospects. In 1860, for example, when an article in *Emigranten* (The Emigrant) praised Blue Earth County's attributes, subsequent issues contained inquiries about land there. The reply of a Linden settler undoubtedly in-

fluenced some to go to this region near the big bend of the
Minnesota River. Thus, while
the early communities remained
heavily Norwegian, the addition
of migrants from various places
in Norway combined with newspapers and other pan-Norwegian agencies to bring about the
gradual loss of Old Country regional exclusiveness.[19]

Big Grove and Spring Grove
faced these changes with little

Linden Lutheran
Church in Linden
Township in
Brown County
on a snowy day
in 1962

overt conflict. Other communities were not so fortunate.
In one, tensions developed between a group of Hallings,
who were in the majority, and people from the Trondheim
region, who constituted a tiny minority. It seemed to at
least two Trønders that the Hallings "kind of liked to have
the upper hand" and that the Halling kids in the parochial
school asserted their "superiority" over the others. Such
tensions were often tied to socioeconomic differences,
since the regional group that arrived first frequently ac-
quired greater wealth and status. Certain periods also involved bitter theological disputes among Norwegians,
which led one scholar to assert that if rural travelers "saw
two churches close together, preferably one on each side of
the road, they were sure to be in the heart of a Norwegian
settlement."[20]

During the early period such settlements were usually
situated in or near wooded areas and on streams or lakes,
for the Norwegians regarded the prairies as less fertile
because they lacked trees. Moreover, since there were no
trees, how would one build a house or secure fuel, and
what would break the force of the winds to provide protec-
tion during storms? The myth of the Great Plains as a
desert led Norwegians as well as other groups to fear the

treeless areas. It remained for Paul Hjelm-Hansen to convince his fellow countrymen that the prairies were indeed desirable.[21]

Hjelm-Hansen arrived in the United States in 1867 at the age of 57. An experienced newspaperman, he went to work for *Fædrelandet og Emigranten* (The Fatherland and the Emigrant), a Norwegian American journal published at La Crosse, Wisconsin. In a series of articles Hjelm-Hansen "emphasized the danger in so many of the emigrants remaining in the city to which their train ticket had taken them." Reflecting the Norwegian penchant for life on the soil, he argued that the surplus labor available in the cities would prevent workers from getting ahead and keep them forever poor. Life as a farmer in Minnesota, he said, was the best option. Lars K. Aaker of Alexandria, a legislator who was also president of the Scandinavian Emigrant Society, organized in 1869, was impressed by Hjelm-Hansen's warnings. Through Aaker the journalist was appointed by Governor William R. Marshall in 1869 as a special agent to encourage Norwegian settlement in Minnesota areas where government land was still available.[22]

Traveling about the state in the summer of 1869, Hjelm-Hansen became "particularly enthusiastic" about the lands of the Red River Valley, which he thought "were best for the Scandinavian immigrants." In dispatches carried by Norwegian-language papers in Minneapolis and La Crosse, he predicted accurately that the area would within ten years be settled by Scandinavians. Hjelm-Hansen's advocacy, coupled with the penetration of the St. Paul and Pacific Railroad into the area in the early 1870s, was instrumental in encouraging the migration that made the Red River Valley the third major Norwegian settlement area in the state.[23]

Following the patterns already described for the southeast, groups from various earlier Norwegian regions took up land on the fertile prairies of the valley. In 1870, for example, people who had emigrated originally from Telemark read Hjelm-Hansen's reports, left Mound Prairie in Houston County, and traveled for two months to reach the Red River Valley. With the help of several earlier settlers, they found satisfactory land on the Buffalo River in Clay County northwest of Glyndon. The first winter was long, but life was brightened by the arrival of one or two letters a week from neighbors and friends in Houston County as well as of the magazine *Ved Arnen* (By the Hearth) published at Decorah, Iowa. In 1871 news came from a former next-door neighbor in Houston County announcing that he was planning to move to the valley. By June 1871, 34 more Telemarkings had arrived from Mound Prairie. "Now we had quite a settlement . . . ," one of them recalled, "and the funny part of it was that all of these settlers . . . here so far had emigrated from the same district in Old Norway, and that was the cause of . . . this Township being named after Moland Prestegield Fyresdal, Norway." To this day Moland Township is peopled by Norwegian Americans.[24]

Major settlement of the Red River Valley got under way in 1871 as wagon trains slowly moved to the open lands. Levi Thortvedt, one of the early Moland Township Norwegians, could remember the passing of as many as 20 trains of covered wagons a day, with cattle and sheep driven along behind. The

Red River Valley artist Orabel Thorvedt drew *Gamle Joran* (Old Joran) in pen and ink in the 1930s. The subject was a great-grandmother she never met, who crossed the Atlantic in 1861 as a grandmother and later accompanied her son and his family and neighbors on the long trek from Houston County to the Buffalo River near Moorhead.

1875 state census reported that about 55% of the foreign-born residents and 30% of the total population of Polk and Clay Counties had emigrated from Norway. Many of these people had moved from southeastern Minnesota, as had the Thortvedt party in 1870. In the next decade the Northern Pacific and Great Northern railroads became important, carrying thousands of immigrants throughout the valley and into the Dakotas. In Marshall County, for example, Norwegians followed the railroad rights of way to concentrate near Warren, Argyle, and Stephen and in New Folden Township, where the Marshall County Skandinaviske Mutual Fire Insurance Company had its headquarters. Later, about the turn of the century, more emigrated directly from Norway, until by 1905 some 57.5% of the people of Marshall, Clay, Norman, and Polk Counties had either been born in Norway or were the children of those who had.[25]

The Red River Valley was the last Minnesota agricultural region to be developed as well as that most heavily settled by Norwegians. The four counties of Clay, Marshall, Norman, and Polk exhibited at least 84 Norwegian place names compared to only 19 in Fillmore and Goodhue Counties in the southeast. Norman County in fact may have been named for the many Norse or "Norman" residents. Later they also spread into nearby Red Lake, Grant, Pennington, Kittson, and Roseau Counties.

Because they were frequently the earliest and the most numerous group, Norwegians established the valley's churches and often dominated its businesses and local affairs. To the northeast in Badger, Roseau County, for example, the Norwegian-owned Scandinavian-American Bank served both Norwegians and Swedes. In Thief River Falls in Pennington County, the local chapter of the Sons of Norway was instrumental in convincing the school board to add a Scandinavian-language course in the high school. During the anti-immigrant hysteria of World War I,

The doughnuts (or sandwiches) and cold drink probably disappeared quickly one summer day around 1900 when two generations of Norman County farmers cut their wheat crop at the Carl Krogstad farm. They used a McCormick reaper pulled by a four-horse team and had to tie the shocks by hand. The identified men are Carl Krogstad, Martin Olson, and Henry Storslie. Mrs. Carl Krogstad and her daughter Anna Olson brought the welcome refreshments to the workers.

Sheriff Ole A. Rice of Roseau County, himself of Norwegian descent, assured all foreign-born residents that "they need not fear invasion of their rights" or confiscation of their property. The predominance of Norwegians permitted the maintenance of various Norwegian cultural elements and the persistence of the language in portions of the Red River Valley into the 1970s and 1980s. The areas of Minnesota where the largest proportion of people who identify their ancestry as Norwegian in the 1990 census indicates their continued dominance in three regions of the state.[26]

To be sure, Norwegian Americans settled in all of Minnesota's major agricultural regions. Whether they took land in the hilly, wooded southeast, the lake-filled Park Region, the flat, treeless plains of the Red River Valley, or the rolling prairies of southern and southwestern Minnesota, they were fulfilling what was perceived at the time as a widespread Norwegian desire to farm. Speaking in 1916, Nicolay A. Grevstad, former editor of Chicago's influential

Ragna Rekkedahl and Martha Aarseth Slettedahl butchered a pig near Echo in 1915. Martha's children looked on from the farmhouse porch as the blood drained into a galvanized tub. Norwegian American Ole Aarseth photographed many such scenes of rural life.

newspaper *Skandinaven* (The Scandinavian), stressed the Norwegian immigrant's propensity to make "a bee-line from the little plot of ground on a hillside in Norway to the princely 160 acres waiting for him in the west," where he reaped "a rich reward." According to Grevstad, at that time foreign-born Norwegian American farmers owned an estimated 11,000,000 acres in the United States worth about $650,000,000. One-third of them lived in Minnesota. And the well-known Norwegian love of the soil carried over to the second generation, for even more of its members (54.3%) farmed than did the firstcomers. Moreover, a larger percentage of them remained rural dwellers than of any other ethnic group. In 1920, 52% of the Norwegian born and 65.4% of their descendants resided in rural areas of the United States.[27]

As Minnesota's portion of the Red River Valley filled up, Norwegian farmers headed farther west to North Dakota, Montana, Washington, and the Canadian prairies. Spring Grove again reflected the general pattern, as 100 residents joined a colony that set out for North Dakota in the summer of 1886. The early Norwegian exodus had begun in part as an attempt to escape urbanizing Norway. So many Norwegian immigrants flocked to the fertile farmlands of the Midwest that by 1910 they were the most agriculturally inclined ethnic group in the nation. Many were able to live a rural life that would have been denied

The town band, dressed in white jackets and caps, in front of Fladager's false-fronted store on Spring Grove's main street for the first homecoming celebration in 1907. Chris Engell and his son were the likely photographers.

them had they remained in Norway. Ironically, however, Norwegian immigrants saw greater urbanization in the new land than at home. While about half of the Norwegian born and 63% of their children lived in rural America in 1900, in Norway nearly two-thirds were still rural dwellers—a proportion made possible by the numbers who had emigrated from the Old Country in the 19th century. Even in Clay County in the heart of the Red River Valley, the number of Norwegians living in villages increased while those on farms declined between 1885 and 1895. By no means did all Norwegian immigrants to the state choose to farm. Urban areas—especially the Twin Cities for those in the Upper Midwest—began to offer more occupational opportunities as industries grew and good land for farming became scarcer.[28]

Norwegian Americans also worked as lumberjacks in the pine forests of northern Minnesota, where they might have earned $25 to $30 a month in the cold winter seasons of the 1880s. Others became part of the small community of Duluth, which in 1870 numbered 3,131 souls of whom 242 were Norwegians. By 1900, more than 7,500 native-born and foreign-born Norwegians were listed in the city. Some of the men became fish merchants there, while

The fishing boat *Grace J* sliced through ice floes in the Duluth harbor in 1915, loaded with bags of frozen herring from the Lake Superior fisheries. The boat was owned by the Norwegian American firm H. Christiansen and Son of Duluth, a company that did business in fish and fishery supplies and handled mail-order shipments of fish to customers throughout the Midwest.

others used their considerable skills, experience, and Norwegian methods to pioneer commercial fishing along the north shore of Lake Superior in the 1870s and 1880s. Concentrated in such small, predominantly Norwegian villages as Tofte and Hovland, Norwegians increased from nearly 50% of the commercial fishermen along the North Shore and in Duluth in 1895 to between 80% and 90% of the 276 people in that occupation in 1920. Catching largely herring that could be sold to their countrymen throughout the Midwest, these immigrants subsisted on a combination of fishing and farming, maintaining a lifestyle that had its roots in the Old Country. Late in the 19th century and early in the 20th, other Norwegian immigrants arrived in northern Minnesota to work in the iron mines. There they found not only ready employment but also a chance to move up in the mining company hierarchies.[29]

Urbanization in Norway was reflected in altered emigration patterns. Beginning in the mid-1880s Norwegian emigration was no longer composed primarily of peasant families. Like the urban centers of the United States, Norway's cities were providing more work opportunities as industrialization raised the country's standard of living. Its gross national product increased by 150% in the 40 years before World War I, while its population grew only 35%. But Norwegian cities not only received in-migrants, they also sent emigrants abroad: more than half the Norwegians who arrived in the United States between 1900 and 1910 were unmarried city dwellers. Nearly two-thirds were men between the ages of 15 and 25. Their reasons for emigrating were still largely economic, but fewer intended to become permanent residents of the New World. Where once the immigrants sailed aboard a creaking wooden ship on an Atlantic crossing that took months, they could now make the trip more swiftly, safely, and cheaply on comfortable steamships. Lower fares made the journey more affordable for larger numbers of people. They could go to Minneapolis for a few years, earn higher wages in Minnesota despite Norway's increasing standard of living, accumulate funds to invest in Norway, and then return as three-fourths of the remigrants to Norway did in 1920 after a stay of from two to nine years abroad. In short, the

Norwegians gathered at the depot in Lanesboro to embark on a visit to their homeland, about 1910.

later Norwegian immigrants, like those from southern and eastern Europe, did not intend to remain for life; they could more easily go back to the homeland, and many did.[30]

The Urbanization of Norwegian Americans

Immigrants who arrived in the 1890s and early 1900s gravitated to the cities, joining Norwegian Americans who moved in increasing numbers from the countryside. It was in this period that Minneapolis assumed its pre-eminence as the country's major Norwegian metropolis. Calling it the second largest Scandinavian city in the world, Lincoln Steffens wrote in 1903 that Minneapolis consisted of "a Yankee with a round Puritan head, an open prairie heart, and a great, big Scandinavian body."[31]

To be sure, Norwegian immigration to the Twin Cities of Minneapolis and St. Paul had begun much earlier. The St. Paul Norwegian community dates from the 1850s and that of Minneapolis from shortly after the Civil War. Between 1865 and 1873, the migration from the countryside and directly from Norway fostered the first distinct Scandinavian commercial districts, the initial Scandinavian secular societies, and the church congregations that became the basis for the urban church. These institutional developments provided the framework for the Norwegian community that eased the adjustment to urban life when the major influx of immigrants occurred between 1880

Ole Draxten, a carpenter and immigrant from Trøndelag, built this house for his family at 1802 2nd St. North in the North Minneapolis Norwegian community. He also built the two houses behind it to rent to other Norwegian immigrants. Pictured on the porch in the early 1880s are his wife Kari and two of their children. Not pictured was their son Bersvend, a founder and first president of the Sons of Norway.

and 1890. In 1880, 11.3% of the state's total population but only 5.3% of its Norwegians lived in the Twin Cities. Soon, however, they constituted the third largest foreign-born group in Minneapolis after the Swedes and the British, increasing fivefold in ten years. By 1890 Minneapolis had replaced Chicago as the principal destination of Scandinavian immigrants to the United States. By then Minneapolis and St. Paul included almost 23% of all Minnesotans and 16% of the Norwegian born. The Norwegians were urbanizing rapidly, but their fellow Minnesotans continued to flock to the cities at a greater rate. In absolute numbers there were 3,315 foreign-born Norwegians in the Twin Cities in 1880; the figure was 16,145 ten years later. By 1910 Minneapolis alone had 16,401, nearly 16% of all the Norwegian born in the state.[32]

According to one author, Norwegians in 1914 controlled 4 of the city's 27 banks, 13 of 26 musical organizations, 15 of 100 newspapers and periodicals, and 23 of 195 churches, while several of the 110 hotels were Norwegian-run, and 37 of 500 doctors were Norwegian. Norwegian

Beard's Block, Minneapolis, shown here in 1912 (left side of street), was known informally as "Noah's Ark." Noted Norwegian American author Ole E. Rølvaag wrote about it in his urban novel, *Boat of Longing*. The three-story building provided decent low-cost housing, with gas, running water, privies, and woodsheds, for poor working families.

and other Scandinavian merchants in Minneapolis were centered on Washington Avenue South. About 1880 their grocery stores, undertaking parlors, and furniture showrooms were concentrated at or near the corner of 11th Avenue South and Washington Avenue, within walking distance of the Norwegian residential community. The latter included "Noah's Ark," a 60-apartment building covering an entire square block at 12th Avenue and 2nd Street South. As they did in rural Minnesota, new arrivals frequently lived with earlier immigrants until they found work. Whereas some worked in the nearby flour mills and sawmills, Norwegian men concentrated in small-scale craft industries and in the construction trades, and women usually worked as domestic servants and dressmakers. Work and residence often were defined by common Norwegian background. As one put it, "It sometimes happened that families which had been close neighbors in Norway became next door neighbors in Noah's Ark."[33]

During the 1880s the Norwegian enclave shifted farther up Washington Avenue to Cedar Avenue, later known as "Snoose Boulevard" because of the large consumption of snuff (called snoose) by its Scandinavian residents. This development was hastened by the establishment of the Scandia Bank in 1883 on the corner of Cedar and 4th Street South. To be near the new bank, many Norwegian merchants relocated in the Cedar-Riverside area, and soon nearly all the businesses there were operated by Scandinavians, many of them Norwegians. The community continued its southward movement, so that in later years South Minneapolis, predominantly Swedish, also became the major domain of Norwegian Americans and their institutions, although some were also to be found in other sections of the city.[34]

Certain patterns of urban settlement were much like rural ones. Relatives and friends often lodged together in the same households, and remittances eased the cost of making the journey to Minnesota. But the Minneapolis Norwegian community differed in several important ways from its rural Minnesota counterparts. For one thing, even the most compact block of Norwegians in the city mingled with other nationalities, occupations, and classes. In the 1890s Ward 11, stretching along the Mississippi from 6th Street to 24th Street South, contained more Norwegians than any other. Nevertheless in 1895 they made up only 15.9% of the population. As a result, Norwegians were more likely to meet people from other ethnic groups than they were in a homogeneous rural settlement like Spring Grove. Recent research nonetheless indicates that apart from Swedes or Danes, members of the Norwegian community associated very little with members of other ethnic groups outside of school or work.

Although more Norwegian Americans resided in Minneapolis, the St. Paul community nonetheless was the earliest settlement in Minnesota, and it remained significant throughout the 20th century. Norwegians were charter members of Scandinavian Methodist and Lutheran congregations in the 1850s that predate any churches of Scandinavian or Norwegian origin in Minneapolis. From 1900 onward, moreover, Ramsey County had the third largest urban Norwegian community in the nation. Historian

Even city-dwelling Norwegian immigrants like Norwegian-born Organ Gundersen, who left his life as a sailor to immigrate to St. Paul, apparently had an interest in farming. The long-time janitor at St. Paul's Schuneman and Evans department store was pictured reading *The Farmer* newspaper, about 1922.

David Mauk, in his study of Norwegians in the Twin Cities, determined that residential clusters of immigrants and their children first developed on St. Paul's East Side and in the Mount Airy section, whose alderman in the mid-1890s was Norwegian-born Johan Larsen. As the city grew, Norwegian American settlements extended to areas near Lake Phalen, the Midway, and Roseville. In large part because of the migration from outlying regions, the proportion of those of Norwegian descent did not peak until 1960.[35]

Many of the secular organizations in the Twin Cities in which Norwegians took part were Scandinavian rather than exclusively Norwegian. Among those listed by a local historian of Minneapolis were the Scandinavian Labor and Benefit Society, the Scandinavian Lutheran Temperance Society, the Scandinavian Old Settlers Society, and the Scandinavian Brass Band, as well as numerous singing, athletic, and dramatic groups. Ethnic labels were often imprecise in urban areas; the same writer recalled a club, known as Den Norske Gutteforening (Norwegian Boys' Association), which flourished in his childhood neighborhood. To its members, he said, all non-Scandinavian children were referred to as "Irish," while members of the Norwegian club were regarded as "Swedes" by the non-Scandinavian residents. As the community grew and as diplomatic tension increased in Scandinavia, however, Norwegians increasingly shunned "pan-Scandinavian" organizations in favor of groups that were entirely Norwegian in origin.[36]

While the city seems to have blurred national origins, especially in the early years of settlement, its greater occupational and economic diversity was a powerful factor in creating more pronounced class differences. The duties of a farm owner and his hired hand were often similar, but in the city a Norwegian might be a common laborer or a bank president. It is unlikely that the members of the Scandi-

"Temperance veterans" gathered at the Betania [Bethany] Church, Minneapolis, for a meeting in 1925. The group may have been a member of the National Total Abstinence Union, organized around 1890 to promote temperance among the Norwegians of the Upper Midwest.

navian Labor and Benefit Society, which published *Arbeidets Ridder* (Knights of Labor) in 1886–87 and became a unit of the national labor organization of the same name, associated regularly with members of the Scandia Club, an exclusive Scandinavian group formed in the mid-1880s. When singer Christina Nilsson visited the city from Europe in 1886, her reception was "an exclusive affair" attended by the Scandinavian "high life," who deliberately failed to invite large numbers of working-class Norwegians.[37]

Further diversity in the Norwegian community was provided in the 1880s and 1890s by a lively group of intellectuals in Minneapolis. Among them were Kristofer N. and Drude Janson and Knut Hamsun. Janson, author and Unitarian minister who founded several congregations during his 12 years in the state, was sympathetic to such then-radical ideas as Socialism and the "social gospel." His wife, Drude, was a novelist and an ardent feminist. Hamsun, who lived for a time with the Jansons in the 1880s, returned to Norway, where he, too, became a well-known author and the winner of a Nobel prize for literature. A frequent correspondent and mentor of the group was Bjørnstjerne Bjørnson, iconoclastic writer, poet, and champion of causes, whose career would bring him world fame. Bjørnson spent a short time lecturing in the United States in 1880–81 and came to know the Janson circle in Minneapolis.[38]

As in rural areas, factions of the Norwegian American urban community violently disagreed over the course they should follow. The intellectuals, for example, were regarded with disdain by Lutheran church people because of the Unitarianism of the Jansons and their associates. Both of those groups, however, felt the "saloon element" to be disreputable and manipulable by machine politicians. In addition to ethical cleavages, regional differences split Twin Cities Norwegian Americans. The smaller North Minneapolis enclave, for example, regarded their countrymen in South Minneapolis as arrogant and elitist.[39]

This is not to say that the Lutheran church was not a powerful force in urban Norwegian American society. Yet again, however, one perceives differences between the city and the countryside. Historian Todd Nichol has shown how the congregation of Our Savior's Lutheran Church in Minneapolis grew and moved from the central city to a residential neighborhood near the city limits. As new churches were built whose exteriors reflected their members' adaptation to American life, their interiors early on illustrated a persistence of ritual practice. Yet the trappings of a Norwegian American folk church were slowly abandoned so that by the 1970s, the interiors also reflected a near complete abandonment of the Norwegian heritage.[40]

The Norwegian Lutheran church was complemented and sometimes challenged by the fraternal society, which crossed economic, class, and occupational lines. Like the Lutheran churches of rural and urban areas, the fraternal society in the cities provided a place to meet and exchange news. Like the early churches, too, lodges were often formed by immigrants who hailed from the same region in Norway. Such was the case with the Sons of Norway, one of the largest and best-known Norwegian American groups in 2001, which had its beginnings in a small Norwegian concentration in North Minneapolis in 1895. Of its 18 founders at least nine were born in the Trøndelag district of Norway and six were from the parish of Selbu there. Begun in a period of severe national financial panic, the group provided insurance and fostered Norwegian culture in the United States. At the same time later lodges came into being in South Minneapolis near the core of the city's Norwegian settlement, the organization also spread to other communities. Both its fraternal and insurance purposes retained their importance.[41]

Nevertheless the Sons of Norway remained an urban institution. Distrust of "city slickers" selling insurance and of "secret societies" was so great a deterrent to securing a

Minde fra Hallingesterne, i Spring Grove, juni 12, 13, 14, 1912

Cartoonist Peter Rosendahl, a Spring Grove area farmer, drew a strip called "Han Per and Han Ola" that was published in the Norwegian-language *Decorah Posten*. He also drew cartoons to commemorate homecomings and *bygdelag* gatherings in Spring Grove. This is a souvenir from the 1912 Hallinglag *stevne*, making fun of Hallings' predilection for drawing their knives even while dancing the challenging men's dance called the *halling*. There are at least 12 knives in this cartoon.

large following in the countryside that in 1903 its general secretary warned against organizing lodges in small places. Instead the rural counterparts of such secular organizations were the *bygdelag* (district societies) composed of immigrants from particular areas in Norway, such as Valdres or Sogn. These two parallel lines of development produced occasional clashes between those who wished to maintain the rural Norwegian culture represented by the *bygdelag*, and those who wished to become part of the more urbanized, pan-Norwegian heritage represented by the Sons of Norway. It should be noted, however, that the *bygdelag* were also active in the cities; they continued to function there and in rural areas in 2001.[42]

Institutional Development

The movement of Norwegian immigrants to the city also influenced the social and cultural emphases of community development. The increasing numbers of Norwegian Americans demanded more efficient and often larger institutions, while improved standards of living made possible a more varied supply of goods and services. As a result, the Minnesota Norwegian American community produced not only church synods and colleges, but newspapers, political organizations, literature, and art. The development of this cultural structure did not mean that organizational conflicts ended. Indeed disagreements among those with varying theological, class, occupational, and political viewpoints continued to occur and likely increased within that structure.

A case in point can be found in the Norwegian Lutheran church. In 1914 Waldemar T. Ager, the editor of a Norwegian-language newspaper, maintained that the "large and affluent Norwegian-American family had only two children, and both were well nourished. The two were church and politics." Strong, sometimes violent, controversies fre-

The Ladies Aid of Immanuel Lutheran Church, Hendrum, Norman County, went to a photo studio, perhaps A. T. Thorson's Photo Gallery, for this 1890s picture. The married women church members usually made up its ladies aid, which provided sociability with other women and worked hard to raise funds for the church's needs and for its missions.

quently raged over the first "child," the church. Coming from an at least nominally united state church in Norway, Lutheran Norwegians in the United States encountered a new religious environment. Not only was there no established state church, but church and state in the United States were separated. Unaccustomed to religious freedom, Norwegian Americans created what one Lutheran pastor likened to "a more vivacious daughter. . . . She also has some bad habits because she feels so free and is not yet used to her freedom." One result of this freedom is that Norwegian Lutherans quickly developed their own religious organizations and split into synods in what one scholar called "the first enterprise that can be called Norwegian-American."[43]

The synods reflected differing theological viewpoints rooted in both the Norwegian and American cultural landscapes. The Evangelical Lutheran Church in America, which emphasized the "low church," pietistic teachings of Hans Nielsen Hauge, was founded in 1846. The views of the state church of Norway were evident in the Norwegian Evangelical Church in America (later referred to as the Norwegian Synod), which was founded in 1853. Before long disagreements over the degree of "low church" tendencies,

the relations of Norwegian Lutherans with other nationalities, and personal politics resulted in the creation of additional synods. By 1876 there were five synods in the United
States, and "each charged the others with failure to represent the true teaching or spirit of Lutheranism." Whereas
the opportunity to create their own religious organizations reflected a discord among Norwegian Lutherans, it is
likely that the multiplication led to a stronger Lutheranism among Norwegians. The possibility to join a church
that reflected one's personal theological proclivities kept
many in the Lutheran fold who otherwise, like Swedish
Americans, might have joined such churches as the Baptists or Methodists in greater numbers.[44]

Theological conflict accompanied religious diversity.
Already in the 1860s the Norwegian Synod was shaken by a
debate over slavery. What became a larger controversy
emerged over the doctrine of election or predestination
that rocked the high-church Norwegian Evangelical Synod
in the 1880s. The issue, briefly stated, was over how much
influence the individual had in his or her own salvation.
Despite its seeming abstract nature, the debate absorbed
first the clergy and then the parishioners. "They argued
predestination in the saloons, with their tongues," it was
said, "and settled it in the alley with their fists." The social
cleavages of varying Norwegian origins often underlay the
theological divisions. Before it was over, 92 congregations
in Minnesota alone were involved, and in the tumult 23 of
them split to form new churches. The latter then united
with two other synods to establish the United Norwegian
Lutheran Church in 1890. Over time, however, a movement toward union developed, which culminated on June 9,
1917, when the Hauge Synod, the Norwegian Evangelical
Synod, and the United Church officially merged to form
the Norwegian Lutheran Church in America. In 1930 in
Minneapolis the Norwegian church joined some other Lutheran groups to become the American Lutheran Church.[45]

With so many Norwegian congregations sprouting in the Midwest, early pastors decided that some means of educating a clergy were needed on American soil. Norwegian American colleges, a second major institutional development, were thus given impetus by the various Lutheran groups. In 1857 the Norwegian Evangelical Synod endorsed a recommendation for the establishment of a Norwegian professorship at Concordia Seminary, a German-Lutheran school in St. Louis, Missouri. When the German Lutherans declined to take a stand against slavery during the years before the Civil War, however, Norwegian Lutherans in 1861 formed their own seminary, which became Luther College in Decorah, Iowa.[46]

The numerous synods, each desiring a place where the "true" doctrine would be taught, went on to found four other surviving Norwegian American schools in Minnesota. St. Olaf College in Northfield had its beginnings in 1874 as an academy under the leadership of the Reverend Bernt J. Muus. By 1886 it was being transformed into a college, eventually sponsored by the United Church. Augsburg Seminary moved from Marshall, Wisconsin, to Minneapolis in 1872; by 1897 in another of the many splits Norwegian Lutheranism was prey to, the Lutheran Free Church was organized with Augsburg College as its institution of

A view of the Hauge Synod Seminary in Red Wing about 1907

R.W.S.

learning. Concordia College in Moorhead began as an academy affiliated with the United Church in 1891. By 1914 it, too, had become a four-year college. Red Wing Seminary was founded in 1879 to serve the Hauge Synod. In 1903 it added a college, which merged with St. Olaf in 1917. The same year its seminary merged with Luther Theological Seminary, which had been started in St. Paul in 1900 by the United Church. Moreover, through the urging of Truls Paulson, a Norwegian serving in the legislature from Spring Grove, a Scandinavian department was started at the University of Minnesota in 1884.

Although many were founded to educate pastors, the church schools quickly evolved into colleges where Norwegian Americans, whether working toward the ministry or not, could find liberal educations. The desire of Norwegians to invest heavily in education spurred them in this direction. One Lutheran leader was amazed at how ready Norwegian parents were "to sacrifice and to suffer that their children may have an education." He "actually saw," he said, "large families living in sod shacks on the open prairie" who were sending a boy or girl to Concordia College at Moorhead.[47]

A third major institution developed by the early immigrants was the Norwegian-language press. Like the synods, the press functioned as what one historian called a "steadying point . . . to weld these people together in common interests, to give reality to the geographically nebulous concept of a 'Norwegian America.'" Initially the founding of healthy newspapers among the Norwegians was difficult. The immigrants were poor, and few had regularly read papers in Norway. The earliest one in the United States was *Nordlyset* (Northern Light), launched at Norway, Wisconsin, in 1847. After the Civil War, however, their growth accelerated. Between 1865 and 1914 some 400 to 500 Norwegian-language newspapers and magazines existed at one time or another.[48]

The first of at least 115 such periodicals known to have been published in Minnesota was *Folkets Röst* (People's Voice) issued in St. Paul in 1857–58. The last of them, *Minnesota Posten* (Minnesota Post), ran from 1897 until it closed its doors in Minneapolis in 1979. At least 45 journals were headquartered in Minneapolis over the years, 10 in St. Paul, and 8 in Fergus Falls. Among the longest-lived Minneapolis papers and magazines were: the weekly *Budstikken* (The Messenger) 1873–94, which then merged with *Fædrelandet og Emigranten* (The Fatherland and the Emigrant) to form *Minneapolis Tidende* (Times), which began as a daily in 1887 and continued into the 1930s; *Folkebladet* (The People's Paper) 1880–1930, *Nye Normanden* (The New Norseman) 1894–1922, *Skandinavisk Farmer Journal* 1883–1910, *Ugebladet* (The Weekly Paper) 1886 or 1890 to 1929 or 1931, and *Ungdommens Ven* (The Youth's Friend) 1890–1916. The last merged with *Kvindens* (The Women's) *Magasin* in 1919 to form *Familiens* (The Family's) *Magasin,* which ceased publication in 1928. St. Paul's *Nordvesten* (The Northwest) ran from 1881 to 1907, *Ugeblad* (Weekly Paper) of Fergus Falls, which was sometimes spelled *Ukeblad,* from 1882 to 1946, and Duluth *Skandinav* from 1887 to 1965.[49]

Over the century, newspapers and magazines served the Minnesota Norwegian community not only from these cities but also from bases of varying stability in Albert Lea (5), Crookston (4), Duluth (4), Madison (3), Moorhead (3), Northfield (3), Red Wing (4), Rochester (2), Sacred Heart (3), and St. Cloud (2). More than 20 additional Minnesota towns, including Spring Grove, had at least one Norwegian newspaper.

The immigrant press has been called a "clearing house for immigrant thought as well as a round-robin letter," for it provided both news of Norway and reports from American settlements. These newspapers in fact are the earliest example of Norwegian American literature. This is not to

The mixture of Norwegian and English spoken by first- and second-generation Norwegian Minnesotans is nicely captured by cartoonist Peter Rosendahl in this souvenir of a Spring Grove homecoming celebration. Because many Norwegian immigrants spent time in Spring Grove before moving, the town organized home-comings, the first one occurring in 1907. Since then it has hosted one in each year that ends in seven.

say that they were immediate successes or that they did not face basic challenges. A newspaper editor wrote its readers in January 1856 that "regardless of how much fuel we burn in these expensive times to keep the print shop warm, the paper nevertheless freezes into one lump. The form is frozen to the stone, the ink and the roll have coagulated, and the press operates at half its normal speed." Nonetheless, the press for the immigrants helped preserve and even accentuate ties to the Old Country, while it also served as "a kind of composite America letter . . . for the common people of Norway." Practical articles about various settlements and the availability of land near them served as a link to tie the scattered communities together while at the same time drawing more immigrants to them. "Let them come— not only from the Old World but also from the East. There is room here for them all," trumpeted *Nordisk Folkeblad* (Nordic People's Paper, Minneapolis) on April 2, 1868, expressing an attitude frequently voiced in that period.[50]

The papers also acted as a forum for ideas. The Lutheran church used them to discuss moral and theological questions, including whether a wife owed complete obedience to her husband. As time went on, other topics such as temperance, the virtues of public schools versus Norwegian-language parochial schools, and the transition of immigrants to Americans continued to be debated. *Nordisk Folkeblad*, probably the earliest widely influential Norwegian paper in the state (1868–75), attempted to unite Scandinavians in various causes. As early as 1869 it led a campaign to elect Hans Mattson, a Swede, as Minnesota's first Scandinavian secretary of state. *The North*, an English-language paper published in Minneapolis from 1889 to 1894, was founded by Luth Jæger, a Norwegian married to Hans Mattson's daughter Nanny, to aid in Americanizing Scandinavians there. Other papers, such as *Minneapolis Tidende* and *Reform* (Eau Claire, Wis.) worked to maintain links with the homeland or to help develop a distinctive Norwegian American culture.[51]

More noticeable in later years, however, was the papers' allegiance to the two major parties and to such third-party movements as the Populists or Prohibitionists. At election time political debates filled the pages, relegating other issues to the background. Norwegian editorials tended to support reform and the rights of labor and farmers. The Fergus Falls *Ugeblad*, a Populist journal, "declared that oil and coal lands should be nationalized." Socialist papers in Minneapolis such as *Gaa Paa!* (Forward) and Kristofer Janson's *Saamanden* (The Sower) defended strikers, as did *Nordvesten*, a Republican, business-oriented paper based in St. Paul.[52]

Aided by an active press, politics—Norwegian America's second "child"—was particularly well nourished in Minnesota. Norwegian Americans' prominent place in the state's political pantheon is evident on the grounds of the Minnesota Capitol. Of the three political figures immortalized in statues there, two—Floyd B. Olson and Knute

U.S. Senator Knute Nelson of Alexandria returned to his birthplace near Voss, Norway, in 1899. Nelson emigrated as a boy with his mother, Ingebjørg Haldorsdatter, who struggled with poverty to raise and educate her son. Nelson personified for many of his compatriots the American dream, beginning as a poor immigrant boy and rising to political power.

Nelson—were of Norwegian descent. The careers of these two men point to the diversity of the Norwegian political heritage. Knute Nelson served as a staid Republican congressman in the 1880s, governor in the 1890s, and United States Senator from 1895 until his death in 1923. Maintaining the longest Senate tenure of any Minnesotan thus far, Nelson became increasingly conservative throughout his career. In contrast, Olson, a popular three-term governor during the Great Depression, remarked in 1934, "I am frank to say I am what I want to be. I am a radical."[53]

One way to understand the success of Norwegian Americans as leaders of various parties is to look to the activism that was a part of their heritage. This explanation emphasizes the *bonde* movement, which represented the rural middle class in Norway, as one that lent itself well to political transfer to Minnesota's rural areas. Unlike many European peasant groups, Norway's freeholding *bønder* had never been serfs and "had remained defiantly independent through the centuries." They were represented in Norway's parliament, which they had helped to form, and they did not hesitate to raise their voices as leaders of various reform efforts there. Moreover in Norway they had also gained experience in working together in agricultural cooperatives and other rural communal groups.[54]

In the earliest years of settlement, Norwegians were loyal to both the Democratic and Republican Parties. Following the Civil War, however, Norwegian voters in the United States developed a strong attachment to the Republican Party—the party known for its slogan of "free land, free soil, and free men" and for its role in preserving the Union. By the 1880s, however, Norwegian communities in Minnesota were beginning to support Norwegian candidates and to object to the Yankee dominance of Republican politics, which reflected the urban capitalism of the era rather than communal rural values. In response, Norwegians throughout the Upper Midwest organized Viking Leagues to obtain greater political impact. As the president of the Minnesota League put it in 1899, the immigrants needed "to teach the silk stocking, blue blood Yankees that the Scandinavians are not descendants of the lower conditions of nature."[55]

The first "great political clash" between the Norwegian and Yankee elements in the state's Republican Party occurred in 1882 when Knute Nelson became the first person of Norwegian birth to be elected to the United States Congress. He represented the fifth district of western Minnesota in the House until 1889. Thereafter various political parties found it to their advantage to nominate Norwegian—or Scandinavian—candidates. By 1914 the power of Norwegians to draw votes was well established. From the 1850s to 1914 six from Minnesota had been elected to Congress, 68 had been elected or appointed to judgeships or various other state offices, 259 had served in the Minnesota legislature, and 893 had held county offices. Norwegians had proportionally higher representation in many Minnesota legislatures than did members of other large ethnic groups, such as Swedes and Germans.[56]

With the growth of the Viking Leagues and hard times in the late 19th century, Norwegian allegiance to the Republican Party began to splinter as the party adopted the garb of industrial capitalism and big business. Among the Norwegian farmers of southeastern Minnesota, this new image proved less threatening than it was for those in the Red River Valley. By the closing decades of the century southeastern farmers had shifted from one-crop agriculture to diversified corn, dairy, or livestock farming, which was more easily adaptable to changing economic conditions. For them the Republican emphasis on business was less uncomfortable, balanced as it was by what they viewed as the party's "correct" stand on such moral issues as temperance. For those in the Red River Valley, still largely tied to single-crop wheat farming, the situation was different. Unregulated grain prices and discriminatory railroad rates profoundly influenced the wheat farmer's income and his transportation costs.

Some were attracted to political groups such as the Prohibitionist Party, which adopted Republican Party moral stands but rejected its economic views. More, however, abandoned the Republicans to join first the Farmers' Alliance and later the Populist Party. In 1890, for example, an

The diversity of political activity by Norwegian Americans in Minnesota is demonstrated in this portrait of the township board of Sioux Agency Township, Yellow Medicine County, in 1914. Photographer Ole Aarseth , a Socialist, inscribed his own party affiliation and those of his fellow board members—Arne Arnestad, Sam Gjermonson, and Ben Olds—on the photograph.

estimated 25,000 Norwegian-born Minnesotans voted for Sidney M. Owen, the Farmers' Alliance candidate for governor. Explaining the defection, a Norman County man wrote that "The Republican party started with good principles and the farmers followed," but it had now "ruined us as a class of people, and by putting party before men they have been able to elect millionaires and railroad agents."[57]

To stem the tide, the Republicans in 1892 nominated Norwegian-born Knute Nelson of Alexandria for governor—a tactic that did not set well with all of the voters. One of them wrote Nelson that "The silk stocking element in the Republican party has always opposed you until now. I do not think that they love you now." He added that Nelson had been "selected" to bring in the Norwegian vote, but the "most bitter opposition you will meet will be from Norwegians." But Nelson won, probably with significant Norwegian help. Republican dominance was, however, shattered in the Red River Valley. The Farmers' Alliance-Populist Party remained strong among Norwegians there because many felt the Republican position was inimical to their way of life.[58]

Like the farmers, Norwegian urban dwellers in the Twin Cities also abandoned the Republican Party. In the 1890s and early 1900s some switched to the Democrats, probably thanks to the influence of Norwegian-born Lars M. Rand, a Democratic machine politician and Minneapolis alderman from the Cedar-Riverside area. Others participated in the growth of "agrarian radicalism." In the 1890 election defections from the Republicans to the Farmers' Alliance were (with one exception) most obvious in the heavily Scandinavian wards of Minneapolis. A student of this political phenomenon concluded that "Populism, despite its constant appeals for labor support, apparently received, not a labor vote, but a Scandinavian vote, in Minneapolis and St. Paul— the largest cities in which the Populists made a strong showing."[59]

Significantly, Minnesota's Norwegian Americans tended not to migrate to the Democratic Party in large numbers until well into the 20th century. Whereas some retained their allegiance to the Republican banner and others joined third parties, few felt comfortable with the Democrats. According to historian Lowell J. Soike, this hesitation to become Democrats was largely due to an anti-Catholic strain among Norwegian Americans that alienated them from a party associated with Roman Catholicism.[60]

During this era, Norwegians in the Red River Valley and the Twin Cities retained their penchant for third-party movements, while those in the rural areas of southeastern Minnesota remained predominantly loyal Republicans. After the demise of the Populist Party in 1896, Norwegian Americans in North Dakota and western Minnesota became active in the Nonpartisan League, a radical farmer-labor movement during World War I that led to the development of the Farmer-Labor Party in the 1920s. Under its banners Floyd B. Olson, of an urban and Norwegian background, and Elmer A. Benson, a rural Norwegian American, became successively elected governors of the state from 1931 to 1939.[61] Once many Minnesotans—Norwegian Americans among them—began to accept the New Deal

Governor Floyd B. Olson signed papers while state Senator Andrew O. Devold, Minneapolis, and state representative J. O. Melby, Oklee, and Ole J. Settenvold looked on; all were of Norwegian birth or parentage.

and following the merger of the Farmer-Labor Party with the Democratic Party after World War II, significant numbers of Norwegian Americans finally affiliated with the Democratic Party.

The differing political preferences of Norwegian Americans in these three Minnesota regions can be explained in terms of their reactions to varying economic conditions. But the chronology of immigration and the background in Norway should also be acknowledged. Those in the southeast, who were satisfied with their farming operations, had immigrated earlier, had experienced a longer period of adaptation to American economic and social conditions, and were loathe to leave the Republican Party. Those in the west, on the other hand, saw similarities between the big business monopolies in the United States and the urban-class dominance they had known in Norway. Nurtured on the values of a rural Norwegian lifestyle, Norwegian Americans whose livelihood was threatened by monopoly capitalism revolted and aided in the creation of new grass-roots political parties.[62] Finally, the urban, working-class Norwegian, who was often a migrant from a Minnesota farm, voted for the party he thought best represented his interests. At times this led him to support the forces of agrarian discontent even though he lived in an urban world.

Many of the patterns set in the early years endured. Visible liberal Norwegian Americans such as Hubert H. Humphrey and Walter Mondale carried the Democratic-Farmer-Labor Party into national political prominence in the late 20th century. Although both lost bids for the presidency in 1968 and 1980, respectively, Humphrey and Mondale differed dramatically from other Norwegian Americans who continued to identify with the Republican Party, such as Al Quie, the governor of Minnesota in the 1980s. As late as 2001, Roger Moe, the DFL senate majority leader, and Steve Sviggum, the Republican house speaker, continued to represent the pattern. Moe, elected in 1970,

Coya Knutson of Oklee campaigned for Congress in 1954. She became the first woman to serve in the U.S. House from Minnesota; during her two terms, she worked on legislation to help family farmers.

came of age on a farm near Crookston in the Red River Valley whereas Sviggum grew up on a farm near Kenyon in the southeast. Despite their political differences, both are of Norwegian ancestry and hence both reflect the deep imprint that Norwegian Americans have made on the state. Indeed, the fact that Minnesota has with three exceptions elected governors of Norwegian and Swedish background since 1905 has led one historian to conclude that outside "the Nordic countries there is nowhere in the world where the social development of a State has been determined by Scandinavian activities and ambitions as in Minnesota."[63]

Literature and Art

While emphasizing Norwegian American political and religious contributions, Waldemar Ager went on to blame the "two children"—the church and politics—for depriving Norwegian American literature. He noted that when fiction was mentioned, the answer was "nonsense. Sensible people knew that they had the church and politics—what would one do with books? . . . And so they smothered the brat [of literature], or nearly did." Ager might have overstated this disinterest in literature because Norwegian Americans produced a wide array of literary works varying from popular forms such as America letters and newspapers to high-brow works of drama and literature. Not surprisingly, Minnesota contributed some of Norwegian America's best-known exponents.[64]

One of the earliest pieces of fiction to portray Norwegian American life in the United States, written by Tellef Grundysen of Fillmore County in 1877, was certainly not great literature. Like many others, it portrayed life both in Norway and in the United States and was issued in book form only after it had appeared as a newspaper serial. Early works of fiction tended to concentrate on church issues, temperance, or the rags-to-riches myth of Norwegians in America. Other authors attacked the rich, the Lutheran church, and the Jews. Lars A. Stenholt, for example, produced pulp stories in this vein so popular on trains and newsstands that he is said to have been the only writer of the Norwegian immigrant tradition who made a living from his pen. In time, colleges and literary societies such as the influential Ygdrasil in Madison, Wisconsin, and the Symra Society in Decorah, Iowa, attempted to bring about a flowering of Norwegian American literature. In Duluth, for example, the enduring Aftenro Society promoted interest in Norwegian literature beginning in 1908; it was still functioning in 2000. Output multiplied so that by the mid-1960s about 250 large and small works of fiction and some 120 volumes of poetry had been produced by three generations of Norwegian American authors, writing in Norwegian or in English.[65]

Two famous writers from Minnesota whose Norwegian backgrounds colored their work in diverse ways were Ole E. Rølvaag and Thorstein Veblen. They were born about 20 years apart on different continents, Veblen in Wisconsin in 1857 and Rølvaag in Norway in 1876. The son of a Norwegian immigrant farmer, Veblen was eight years old when the family moved to virgin land near present Nerstrand in Rice County, Minnesota. Rølvaag immigrated to the United States soon after his 20th birthday. By 1901 he was attending St. Olaf College in Northfield, where he would remain as a teacher for most of his life. Veblen had entered Carleton College, also in Northfield, 27 years earlier. His matriculation in that New England-oriented school launched a career closely tied to the Progressive movement of the early 20th century.[66]

Thorstein Veblen, about 1920

From the publication of his first book, *The Theory of the Leisure Class*, in 1899 until his death 30 years later, Veblen remained an acidic critic of American capitalistic society. David Riesman has emphasized this author's "marginality as a second-generation Norwegian, put off and alienated from the parents' parochial culture but without the ability fully to assimilate and accept the available forms of Americanism."

A more convincing explanation, however, may be found in the influence of the Norwegian *bonde* culture of his father. The son's hatred of business, with its "parasitic" system of credit and distribution and its promotion of "conspicuous consumption," can be related to his dislike of the Norwegian urban classes instilled in him by his father. Despite his inability to fit into the Norwegian American settlement at Nerstrand and his education at Carleton College and Yale University, Veblen's Norwegian cultural heritage influenced the development of the economic theory for which he is famous.

Rølvaag's career differed greatly from Veblen's. Educated in Norwegian American academies in South Dakota and Minnesota, he never left Norwegian institutions of learning. Immersed in Norwegian American culture, his novels and short stories dealt with the Norwegian immigrant and his or her difficulty integrating into American society. His most famous book, *Giants in the Earth*, considered by many to be the finest fictional account of the immigrant experience, was published in Norwegian in Oslo in 1924 and in English translation in the United States in 1927.[67]

Rølvaag believed it essential that the immigrants retain their Norwegian cultural backgrounds, for by leaving Norway, he said, they became strangers—"strangers to the people we forsook and strangers to the people we came to." Although he looked upon immigrants in America as "rootless," he was convinced that assimilation was not desirable. If they tried to become Americans, their strong but "hidden" Old Country cultural forms would give way to an emptier society, which, his biographer said, would resemble a "gilded shell." In Rølvaag's apocalyptic vision, denial or neglect of "the heritage of our fathers" would result in a culture without substance, and eventually America would destroy itself. On the other hand, if the immigrants retained their cultures in the new land, America would develop "a future rich in tradition and progressive in spirit."

Ole E. Rølvaag wrote novels about the immigrant experience in the Upper Midwest and was among the founders of the Norwegian-American Historical Association. Here he sits, writing implements in hand, in the backyard of his Northfield home in 1928.

The careers of Veblen and Rølvaag were in many ways as different as day and night. Veblen moved into the Ivy League academic world and did not explicitly write of his Norwegian heritage. Rølvaag devoted his life to the maintenance of that heritage. He celebrated his Norwegianness while Veblen, though moving outside the Norwegian American community, never escaped the assumptions of *bonde* culture passed on to him by his father. In the end, both men were heavily influenced by their immigrant backgrounds.

Notable Minnesotans of Norwegian descent, who were active in painting, sculpture, and music, also reflected a linkage between their heritage and their Minnesota home. Perhaps the most well-known such artist was Herbjørn Gausta, who immigrated from Norway when he was 13. Although he lived in Minneapolis and in rural Fillmore County for most of his life, his work drew upon his memories of his native Telemark. He left Minnesota for art schools in Europe, funded in part by prominent Norwegian Americans, and received a diploma from the Academy of Art in Munich in 1881. He settled in Minneapolis in 1888 where he lived until his death in 1924. Gausta's work, a rich combination of Norwegian and American landscapes, illustrates his facility to move almost effortlessly between Norwegian and American themes. His

In addition to altar pieces, such as the one behind him, Herbjørn Gausta painted landscapes from the area around Harmony, Minnesota, where his parents farmed, and elsewhere in the state. The landscapes on the studio wall are of scenes in Norway.

The budding trees of spring and Norwegian violinist Ole Bull's statue in Loring Park, Minneapolis, presided over a nattily dressed Norwegian a capella men's chorus on May 17, 1930. *Syttende mai,* or the 17th of May, is Norwegian constitution day, a parallel to the American Fourth of July. The statue was restored to its original bronze glory in 2000.

standing in the community is reinforced by about 400 altars that he painted in Norwegian American Lutheran churches. Jacob H. Fjelde, a noted sculptor, whose son Paul followed in his footsteps, immigrated to Minneapolis in 1887. He brought with him the traditional craftsmanship of Norwegian wood carving augmented by study in Copenhagen and Rome. His final work was a statue of Ole Bull, famed Norwegian violinist, which stands in Loring Park, for many years the site of the annual Norwegian constitution day *syttende mai* (May 17) celebrations in Minneapolis.[68]

F. Melius Christiansen, who immigrated in 1888 as a boy of 17, became head of the music department at St. Olaf College in 1903 and retained the post until his retirement in 1944. During his long career (carried on by his son Olaf), he developed the famous choirs that were largely responsible "for having started the a cappella movement in the United States." In his choral work and in the music he composed, Christiansen drew on the treasury of music within the Norwegian Lutheran church and made it accessible to the millions who heard his St. Olaf choirs on their numerous international tours.[69]

F. Melius Christiansen came out of retirement to rehearse the choir in his arrangement of the hymn "Beautiful Savior" in 1951. The Minneapolis concert, to celebrate his 80th birthday, was sponsored by the Minneapolis Symphony. His son, Olaf C. Christiansen, listened in the foreground.

Even more than in the fine arts, Norwegian Americans have placed a great cultural imprint on Minnesota by the transplantation of folk art and folk music traditions. For centuries, Norwegians artists created elaborate wood carvings, wood pieces with beautiful *rosemaling* (rose-painting), ornate folk dress, and haunting folk melodies. They brought these traditions to Minnesota in a variety of ways. Because at the time of the great migration many folk

A Norwegian dance team in colorful traditional costumes at Sacred Heart, 1937

art traditions were already declining in importance in Norway, they did not become integral parts of the Minnesota immigrant community, which itself was adapting to an industrializing American world. Nonetheless, individual artists bequeathed beautiful pieces, many of which were created in Minnesota and survive today at the Vesterheim Museum in Decorah, Iowa. Perhaps the most remarkable work is a wooden altar carved around 1900 by Lars Christianson, who was born in Sogndal in Norway in 1864 and lived in Benson, Minnesota. Likewise, the *bygdedans* (folk dance) traditions of the rural Norwegian regions were carried to Minnesota, but they soon competed with other musical forms, such as the waltz and polka, that were performed by a range of European groups. Nonetheless, a

Farm animals joined the musicians when Thorstein Skarning's Norwegian Hillbillies orchestra performed in 1938. The photo is inscribed in Norwegian "To our old friend Ted Johnson," a well-known Swedish American orchestra leader. Johnson called Skarning's Famous *Norske Orkester* one of America's favorite and Minnesota's most famous Norwegian American old-time dance orchestras.

synergy of older traditions and American innovations fostered an "old-time" music style demonstrated by such groups as Thorstein Skarning and His Norwegian Hillbillies in the 1930s.[70]

In the last half of the 20th century, a revival of folk art occurred both in Norway and the United States. Minnesota artists have energized older traditions as varied as *rosemaling*, Hardanger embroidery, and wood carving, and they have found a ready market for their work among people whether or not they were of Norwegian ancestry. Likewise, ethnomusicologists, such as Philip Nusbaum (who is not of Norwegian ancestry), have worked to recover the tradition of Norwegian folk music in the 1980s and 1990s.[71]

Although such institutions as churches and newspapers, literature, and other arts were initially designed to serve a Norwegian American audience, some developed a

This plate, labeled "Solhaug/St. Paul," was painted by rosemaler Eleanor Ericson of St. Paul probably in the 1950s.

wider following. In so doing, their adaptations have varied greatly. As artists, for example, became less dependent on Norwegian American patronage, the content of their work often changed so that the Norwegian immigrant experience was less emphasized. It is significant, however, that as the content changed, the basic assumptions frequently remained the same. Norwegian roots were usually apparent, whether they lay in the artistic depiction of religious forms or in the revival of Norwegian Lutheran music. Some, like newspaper editors or Lutheran ministers serving predominantly Norwegian American audiences, accepted, as did Rølvaag, the necessity of maintaining the ancestral heritage. Others, perhaps politicians or artists with a more mixed clientele, often remained, like Veblen, so bound to unconscious Norwegian American cultural beliefs and assumptions that their work reflected them even when it was not intended to do so. Still others, such as recent folk artists, consciously utilized and adapted older traditions to appeal to an audience that was not necessarily of Norwegian background but appreciated the migration and adaptation of a tradition. They reflect the varied ways that Norwegians in Minnesota acculturated and how their impact on the state changed.

Acculturation

From the days of settlement, Minnesota Norwegians debated to what degree they should surrender the trappings of their European heritage and replace it with American forms and practices. As it turned out, acculturation did not proceed in a straight line from an extremely retentive Norwegian group in the 1850s to one that valued assimilation in later years. Nor did Norwegian identification necessarily mean that Norwegian Americans did not consider themselves American. Rather, historians in recent years have stressed the way that Norwegian Americans merged

Scandinavian women in national costume, very likely members of the city's Scandinavian Women's Suffrage Association, marched along Hennepin Avenue in a Minneapolis parade for woman suffrage in 1914. Alongside the visible flags of Norway and Denmark, the lead marcher carried a banner asking that women vote on equal terms. The SWSA was organized in 1907.

their identities as *both* Norwegian and American. In fact, the first arrivals expected their folkways to die very quickly. As early as 1845 one predicted that Norwegian-language usage would end "in the second generation." Instead the retention of traditions carried from Norway for a time became more pronounced as immigration continued, and the community grew in wealth and influence, and founded institutions to facilitate the development of a Norwegian American culture. It was in the early 20th rather than in the mid-19th century that Norwegian ethnic consciousness seemed most pronounced. This high point was probably reached just before World War I, but allegiance to nationality group did not continually decline thereafter. Indeed, the Norwegian American identity in Minnesota may have been more self-conscious in 1980 than it was in 1950.[72]

The first quarter of the 20th century marked both the peak of a conscious Norwegian American identity and the beginning of its decline. In 1914 Minnesota's Norwegians vigorously celebrated the centennial of the Eidsvoll Constitution that had signaled Norway's independence from Sweden. After parades in both of the Twin Cities, about 50,000 people—the largest known gathering of Norwegian Americans up to that time—congregated at the Minnesota State Fairgrounds in St. Paul on May 17, Norwegian constitution day. The program featured music, fireworks, and many speakers, but its highlight was Swedish-born Governor Adolph O. Eberhart's recitation of Norway's national anthem in Norwegian. Symbolically the celebration was important to Minnesota Norwegians as a milepost marking "their strength and also the fact of their acceptance as a part of the American nation."[73]

The year 1914 might be arbitrarily taken as a highwater mark of Norwegian American activity in the state. The previous decade had been one of substantial immigration, and numerous organizations had been formed in response to the large influx. Not only were there the lodges of the Sons of Norway and the *bygdelag*, but *Det norske Selskap i Amerika* (The Norwegian Society of America)

Several young women waved Norwegian flags as they enjoyed the festivities of a *syttende mai* celebration in the Twin Cities in 1914.

was founded in Minneapolis in 1903 for the purpose of preserving Norwegian culture in the United States. Furthermore enrollment in Norwegian-language classes was apparently on the upswing. One figure based on reports from 32 of Minnesota's 87 counties indicated that Norwegian was taught in 103 grade and country schools during the 1913–14 school year. But this activity was short-lived. Five years later the state's Norwegians would be much more timid about celebrating their ancestral heritage.[74]

A significant problem in maintaining a Norwegian identity was the changing nature of the immigrant population. Later-arriving Norwegians were better educated and adapted more easily to urbanized America than those of the mid-19th century. More important, the first arrivals were dying off and the second and third generations were maturing. The greater prosperity and education of the immigrants' children pushed Norwegian American institutions to improved intellectual and literary activity, but these young people lacked their parents' personal attachment to Norway. The English language they had been taught in the public schools seemed more natural to them than the Norwegian their parents often insisted on speaking at home. Painful cleavages between generations and breakdowns of communication between parent and child occurred when Norwegian questions received only English answers. Moreover geographical and social mobility worked against the maintenance of ethnic consciousness. Many of those who had achieved success in business after moving to the cities were not conspicuous advocates of an independent Norwegian American culture. Instead they supported integration into the broader American society.

Although 1914 may be regarded as a high point for Norwegian American community life in Minnesota, cracks in the edifice were evident as early as 1890 when the introduction of English-language preaching in the Lutheran church was anonymously suggested in a synod publication. Seven years later another proponent was criticized for addressing a church convention in English. No sermons were preached in English before 1900, but church leaders realized the question would not go away. Between 1905 and 1915 English sermons in the Norwegian Lutheran church rose from 5% to 22%. In 1913 Theodor H. Dahl, president of the United Norwegian Lutheran Church, encouraged "English work," for he feared that without it the churches would lose the third and fourth generations.

The slow, laborious transition from Norwegian to English would probably have been made more gradually had not World War I with its 100% Americanism intervened painfully to speed it up. As they did among other ethnic groups, nosey "Americanizers" intruded upon Norwegian American social, political, and religious life to denigrate hyphenated Americans. The Minnesota Commission of Public Safety, established by the legislature in April 1917, was given near-dictatorial powers to impose conformity on ethnic groups. The agency required the registration of all aliens, resolved that English was to be the "exclusive medium of instruction" in all the state's schools, and banned meetings of any groups suspected of favoring the "idea of peace." Spies were sent to rallies and speeches, with instructions to report any Socialistic, antiwar, and anti-conscription tendencies to their superiors.[75]

While Minnesota's Germans were more harshly repressed, suspicion also fell on Norwegians. In 1917 a spy reported on the activities of a speaker lecturing primarily to Scandinavian audiences, including many Norwegians, in such Red River Valley towns as Fertile, Climax, and Erskine. The Safety Commission also organized a Scandinavian Press Service to watch over the foreign-language press and to provide pro-America tracts for use in the newspapers. Nicolay Grevstad, chairman of the service and a Norwegian American himself, remarked that at its inception in August 1917 some Scandinavian papers "were as little loyal as they found it safe to be." He added that "nearly all have wheeled into line, and some are now aggressively American." Nor was the Norwegian Lutheran church beyond reproach. When O. Morgan Norlie was asked to report on the church and its schools, he attempted to soothe the commission's suspicions by suggesting that the "Norwegian parochial schools are religious schools, not language schools," adding that English was gaining in influence within the church.[76]

World War I hysteria and its coincident militant Americanism put increasing pressure on ethnic communities in Minnesota to renounce their Old World ties. Norwegian Americans, most of whom backed the effort once war was declared, were forced to examine their institutions through the prism of magnified American perceptions, which now viewed any "foreign" activity as suspect. Responding to this pressure, the name of the Norwegian Lutheran Church in America was changed in 1918 to the United Lutheran Church, and Norwegian-language services dropped from 73.1% to 61.2% between 1917 and 1918. Many *bygdelag* gatherings were canceled in 1917, for as one of them (*Nordhordlandslaget*) cautiously explained, "we don't want to give anyone opportunity for misunderstanding, but prove that we are citizens of this country."[77]

The constant doubts thus cast on the virtues of Norwegianness accelerated the transition to American norms. That the period was an aberration in the speed of transition can be seen in the resumption of Norwegian-language church services, which rose from 61.2% in 1918 to 65.7% the following year before beginning a long decline averaging 2.3% a year to 1948. The Norwegian Lutheran Church resumed its original name in 1920, and the Sons of Norway prospered as did numerous other Norwegian groups. But such institutions as the *bygdelag* and the foreign-language press declined. Subscribers to the newspaper *Minneapolis Tidende* dropped from 32,931 in 1910 to 17,000 in 1925.

Unless institutions maintained their utility for the changing needs of the Norwegian American community in Minnesota, they appeared doomed to oblivion.

Some intellectual leaders believed that the period's extreme pressures to conform had sapped the strength of Norwegian American culture. With others of similar mind, Ole Rølvaag in 1919 was instrumental in founding *For Fædrearven* (For the Ancestral Heritage), an organization whose aim was "To awaken ... a deeper appreciation of and love for the great values we have received from our fathers." With Rølvaag as secretary and the Reverend Halvor Bjørnson of Kratka in the Red River Valley as vice president, the society worked for ethnic maintenance. To insinuate that people of immigrant stock were not true Americans "wholly to be depended upon" in wartime, Rølvaag asserted in 1921, was "a virulent contagion" that destroyed their ideals and values. Once again he proclaimed the need to maintain ties to the past in order to create a strong culture in the present. His concern was not widely shared, however, and *For Fædrearven* folded only three years after its inception.[78]

The transition from a Norwegian American culture to what might be called an American Norwegian one affected different groups in varying degrees. After World War I the shift to English continued more gradually in the church and on the street until by 1925 the number of church services in English exceeded those in Norwegian for the first time. In compact rural parishes, the change-over took longer. In addition to the concern expressed by intellectuals like Rølvaag, Lutheran ministers feared the demise of the Norwegian language for both personal and cultural reasons. On the one hand, the prospect of speaking English, which was a foreign language to many of them, was daunting. As early as 1914 the Reverend Johan A. Bergh recorded that Norwegian pastors were "meeting with the unfortunate circumstance that their congregations are very critical with regard to their English." Youths who had attended public schools, he wrote, were prone to criticize "the pastor who uses a word incorrectly or puts an intonation in the wrong place." On the other hand, pastors and elderly church members had difficulty accepting a traditional ritual performed in English. "I have nothing against the English language," one man said, "I use it myself every day. But if we don't teach our children Norwegian, what will they do when they get to heaven?"[79]

One year after the passage of the Immigration Act of 1924, which had signaled a sea change in American immigration policy, the year 1925, like 1914, was marked by a celebration that may serve as a second milepost for Norwegian Americans. To call attention to the centennial of the arrival of the first group of Norwegians in the United States, President Calvin Coolidge spoke to 75,000 Minnesotans, who again gathered at the Minnesota State Fairgrounds. But things had changed since 1914. Now the speeches were predominantly in English, and the crowd heard a series of nostalgic addresses extolling the Norwegian American past as well as an assimilationist future. Perhaps the most symbolic event in the celebration occurred when 500 Norwegian American children, arranged in red, white, and blue clothing, formed a living Norwegian flag and then reversed their capes to transform themselves into an American flag. The lesson was clear: Norwegians, perhaps unlike other nationalities that were immigrating to the United States, could effortlessly assimilate into an American world. Yet as historians April Schultz and Orm Øverland have stressed, Norwegians themselves were instrumental in the creation of this American identity—just as a human flag could be effortlessly transformed from that of one nation to another. When Norwegians observed that they were the real discoverers of America or that Norwegians had helped save the Union during the Civil War, Øverland argues, they were pointing out that their ethnic

A schoolchildren's chorus formed a living Norwegian flag in red, blue, and white at the Norwegian centennial celebration in June 1925. Later in the program they reversed their capes to form an American flag in red, white, and blue.

group was a crucial part of the American—not just the Norwegian American—historical past. As the children of immigrants increasingly used English and as the number of immigrants declined with the new immigration law, the risk in this strategy was that the Norwegians' contributions would be stressed less and less and the American identity would increase. In 1925, too, the Norwegian-American Historical Association was formed with its headquarters at Northfield. Like the centennial celebration, its organization signaled to some the fact that Norwegian America would no longer make history but only write it—in English.[80]

The decades that followed saw further changes in Norwegian American institutions that reflected a growing lack of interest in things Norwegian. Amid the Great Depression, both the Norwegian-American Historical Association and the Sons of Norway reached low points in membership as people failed to pay their dues. That this failure was attributable to poverty rather than disinterest is indicated by the increases recorded by both organizations after that date. In contrast, American xenophobia during World War II focused upon the Japanese rather than the Europeans, so Norwegians escaped the discrimination they had experienced in World War I. In fact, Norway's bravery in the face of Nazi oppression gave added luster to the image of those in America and enlisted their support. Nonetheless, in 1944 the Norwegian church voted to change its name to the Evangelical Lutheran Church, noting that the change was "not born of any wish to repudiate our Norwegian heritage." In 1942 the Sons of Norway decided that the time had come to issue that group's magazine in English rather than Norwegian in order to make the organization more effective. Apparently overwhelming numbers of Norwegian Americans now spoke only English.[81]

Not only had the children of immigrants stopped speaking Norwegian, but fewer and fewer new immigrants were arriving to help keep Norwegian cultural traits alive. Restrictive quotas on immigration, which began in the 1920s, combined with the effects of the Great Depression and World War II to end the mass migrations that had characterized previous periods.

Despite dwindling numbers of immigrants, World War II provoked a flurry of activity in Norwegian America. Minneapolis Norwegians organized the Camp Little Norway Association in 1941, named for the training school of the Royal Norwegian Air Force in Toronto. The national board of the organization was located in Minneapolis. Other groups such as the National Ski Association and the Supreme Lodge of the Sons of Norway joined as special chapters to aid Norway and Norwegians during the war.

When the fighting ended, the association gave way to another organization called American Relief for Norway. Money and clothing were collected by Minnesota Norwegian Relief, Inc., with 3,000 ladies aid societies in the state

On Land — On Sea
In the Air

NORWEGIAN RELIEF, INC.

Norwegian Americans in Minnesota and throughout the U.S. rallied to Norway's cause during World War II, contributing support after Norway was invaded and taken over by Germany. Posters like this one encouraged support for the beleaguered country through donations of clothing, shoes, medicine, and money. Minnesota groups participating included the Camp Little Norway Association, Minnesota Norwegian Relief, Inc., Service Center for Norway, all based in Minneapolis, and in Duluth, the Women's Committee for Norwegian Relief and the Stadheim Lodge #48 of the Daughters of Norway.

participating in the work. Among the organizations that collected money were numerous *bygdelag*, temperance groups, churches, the Sons and the Daughters of Norway, singing and folk-dance groups, the Norwegian-American Athletic Club, and the Progressive Literary Club. From 1942 to 1945 a Service Center for Norway, run by Norwegian American women's groups, also operated in Minneapolis. Through it some 82,000 pieces of clothing were sent to Norway.

Nor was Minneapolis the only place in the state where efforts to aid the Norwegians were organized. In Duluth the Women's Committee for Norwegian Relief, representing 1,000 Norwegian American women in some 20 organizations, was formed to "raise money, buy and distribute materials to be made up for the Norwegian Armed Forces and civilians and to cooperate with other relief agencies." Women in such other northern Minnesota towns as Two

Harbors, Cloquet, Barnum, Carlton, Hibbing, Virginia, International Falls, and Little Fork joined the effort. Women in Northfield also knitted, sewed, and raised money for Norwegian relief through their local branch of *Nordmanns-Forbundet* and the Nordic Arts Club.[82]

Post-World War II saw a changed pattern of immigration, as Norwegians among other nationalities moved to Minnesota to take white-collar jobs, not always intending to stay for extended lengths of time. In the three decades following the war, emigration remained under 3,000 per year, dwindling to less than 1,000 in the late 1960s and 1970s. Only 46,881 Norwegians moved to the United States during this era and many of these returned. The reasons these people had for coming to the United States were, as they had been in the 19th century, primarily economic. But unlike the *bønder* and *husmenn* of earlier years, few of these migrants were attracted to farming. Engineers represented a consistent percentage, following a tradition that brought many of them to the United States temporarily or perma-

Prime Minister Einar Gerhardsen of Norway was introduced at the Minnesota centennial dinner at the Leamington Hotel, Minneapolis, in 1958. The dinner was sponsored by Governor Orville Freeman (left) and the Minnesota Centennial Commission in honor of the delegation of Scandinavian dignitaries who attended the state's festivities. First Lady Jane Freeman applauds at right.

nently since 1879. A second large group represented in the 1950s and 1960s was made up of nurses. Like the previous migration, however, the mid-20th-century one contained numerous family units with a "near balance between the sexes." Over 40% ranged in age from 15 to 29 years.[83]

Relatively few chose Minnesota as their destination. The state ranked second only to New York in number of Norwegian aliens in 1940 with more than 12% of the United States total; nine years later a count of naturalized Norwegians dropped Minnesota behind California and Washington as well. A 1980 study of the postwar migration showed that in 1970 Minneapolis had a relatively large 20% of second-generation Norwegian Americans in the

A large crowd gathered to hear from Princess Astrid of Norway and the Norwegian delegation to the Minnesota centennial celebrations when they visited St. Olaf College in Northfield in May 1958.

United States, but only 10% of those born in Norway. Although the percentage of second-generation Norwegian Americans cannot be calculated in the 1990 and 2000 censuses, there is no reason to believe that the proportions of Norwegians in Minnesota has changed appreciably.

By 1950 the Norwegian America of 1914 was no longer clearly visible in Minnesota. The third and fourth generations considered themselves Americans, spoke English, and increasingly married persons from other ethnic groups. A culture based on class, occupation, or region (such as the Midwest) seemed to have displaced Norwegianness. Like Veblen in his Yankee world, Norwegians may have exhibited certain characteristics—perhaps the cultural traditions of the home such as Lutheranism, a continued predilection for farming, a preference for the professions, or a fondness for certain ethnic foods. But it could be argued that some of these traits were midwestern rather than exclusively Norwegian. This is not to say that a Norwegian identity had ceased to exist. In 1949, in fact, 5,000 people attended the unveiling of a statue of Leif Erikson on the grounds of the state capitol in St. Paul.

Indeed an obituary for Norwegianness in Minnesota in 1950 would have proven premature. In the following decades a growing national interest in "roots" spurred a re-emergence of emphasis on ethnic life.[84] Derived as was much of the so-called new ethnicity from the rising Black national consciousness, a new awareness of their Norwegian heritage began to appear among Norwegian Americans. The causes of this renaissance were at least twofold. First, the revivals of interest in the 1960s were based on a new awareness of the nation's unmelted ethnic diversity. Norwegians as well as other groups began to celebrate a past their parents had been persuaded to believe was undesirable. The second factor was related: the pressures to conform to so-called American or Yankee values had diminished and were now muted.

Picture-taking and music were the order of the day as a large crowd gathered for the dedication of the Leif Erickson statue on the capitol grounds in St. Paul. The date was appropriate: Leif Erickson Day, October 9, 1949, during the Minnesota territorial centennial year. Christ Lutheran Church, a Norwegian American congregation, is visible behind the statue, upper right. In the lower right corner are the caps of a Norwegian male chorus. The Norse Centennial Daughters of St. Paul gave torsk (cod) dinners and conducted other fund-raising events to raise the money for the statue.

The rebirth of awareness of ethnicity among Minnesota's Norwegian Americans differed from older forms of ethnicity. In the past, Norwegians lived their Norwegian folkways, speaking Norwegian on the street and in their churches. Today in a more complex society, Norwegian Americans may speak Norwegian perhaps only at the meeting of a fraternal organization or singing society, and they may participate in traditional folk dances only as a diversion. Other Norwegian Americans cannot speak the

The winter holiday season was a busy time for this lutefisk factory in Golden Valley, Dec. 15, 1971.

language but represent their ethnic allegiance by dutifully eating *lutefisk* and purchasing Norwegian American crafts. This "symbolic" ethnicity is different from an ethnic allegiance based on an immigrant past. The interest of many Norwegian Americans in their ancestral culture is more casual. They are Americans curious about their backgrounds, not Norwegian immigrants trying to become Americans.

The pursuit of Norwegianness in Minnesota in the late

20th century took various forms. In 1980, for example, 63 Norwegian groups cooperated in organizing the first state-wide *syttende mai* (May 17) celebration, which was held in Minneapolis. The parade, studded with Norwegian costumes and American and Norwegian flags, included representatives of several Sons of Norway lodges, at least two *bygdelag*, and an impressive Norwegian men's choral group, as well as the Macalester College Pipe Band of St. Paul in full Scottish regalia, Minneapolis Aquatennial and St. Paul Winter Carnival royalty, and Minnesota-based officials from several Nordic countries, among them the Swedish and Icelandic consuls. Some twenty years later, Guy Paulson, a second-generation Norwegian American, built a replica of a 13th-century wooden stave church located in Vik, Norway. He completed the church at the Hjemkomst Center in Moorhead, which also houses a reproduction of a Viking ship, in 1998 to honor his Norwegian and Christian heritage. Norwegian Americans, many of whom have never been to Norway, are reportedly moved to tears because they are able to see in these structures the roots of their heritage.[85]

This sense of a symbolic ethnicity that, like the Norwegian and American living flag described above, links the ancestral homeland to an American national home is also well illustrated in contemporary Christmas celebrations. As Kathleen Stokker points out, Minnesotans have retained or rediscovered Norwegian or Norwegian American Christmas traditions. Feasting on *lutefisk* and *lefse*, for example, Norwegian Americans can symbolically affirm their ethnic background, just as they remember Christmases of their youth. And whereas *lutefisk* (cod preserved in lye) has fallen out of favor in Norway, Norwegian Americans can rightfully claim that it is (or at least was) authentically Norwegian. Yet their celebration of Christmas also nests Norwegian Americans in a larger Christian American tradition, and their children can enjoy visits to Santa Claus and

Christmas gift giving with their non-Norwegian neighbors. In this sense, Norwegian Americans in Minnesota illustrate their distinctiveness under the umbrella of a festival that many of their neighbors also celebrate.[86]

In addition to Christmas, a flourishing symbolic connection to things Norwegian American is manifest in a series of other activities and affiliations. An attachment to Lutheranism remains as an interest in the Norwegian language grows. Norwegian-language services were conducted every Sunday in 2001 at *Mindekirken,* the Norwegian Lutheran Memorial Church of Minneapolis, one of two such congregations in the United States to do so. This church had an official membership of 270 households, the majority of whom were born in Norway; it sponsored Norwegian classes and was proud to announce that "the kitchen in the basement is just as important as the pulpit upstairs." Cultural skills programs in traditional Norwegian crafts, music, genealogy, and literature were popular with members of the Sons of Norway, whose Minnesota membership has remained relatively steady with some 13,000 members in 1970 and 11,426 in 2001. Not only were individuals interested in Norwegian activities, but whole communities were organizing festivals to celebrate their immigrant heritage. Some, such as the Viking Sword and Turkey Barbeque Day at Ulen in the Red River Valley, reached back to a more ancient past, combining it with typically American food and parades.[87]

Perhaps the best indicator of this vital connection between Minnesotans and their Norwegian past is that more than three-quarters of a million Minnesotans chose to identify themselves as Norwegian American in 1990. This number nearly equaled the entire number of immigrants from Norway to the United States over the course of more than 175 years. It was also equal to about one-fifth of the entire present-day population of Norway. To these Norwegian Americans, we may add those Minnesotans who did not

Norwegians continued to emigrate to Minnesota after World War II, including some of these stalwart supporters of Minneapolis's Norwegian Lutheran Memorial Church, shown leaving the church on Sunday morning and in the church basement kitchen in 1994.

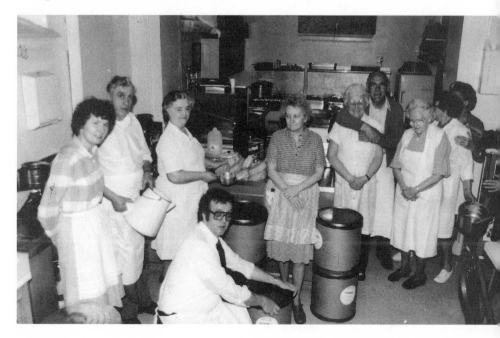

identify themselves as Norwegian but who identify with the Norwegian American cultural past. Together these Minnesotans make their state a richer place and reflect the connections between a past and future observed decades ago by Ole Rølvaag, "We urge a cultural solidarity with the past because we desire that our people shall be made to feel at home in this new land of theirs. . . . We believe that this cultivation of love for home and heritage is the truest Americanization that any citizen may be taught."[88]

Personal Account:
Letter from an Immigrant

by Paul Hjelm-Hansen

Paul Hjelm-Hansen, a native of Bergen, Norway, was an experienced au-thor and journalist before traveling to the United States in 1867. His essays for the Fœdrelandet og Emigranten *(The Fatherland and the Emigrant), a newspaper published in La Crosse, Wis., brought him the attention of Minnesota boosters. In summer 1869, he journeyed through Douglas and Grant Counties to Wilkin and Clay Counties in the Red River Valley and reported on the area's suitability as a new home for Scandinavian immi-grants. He declared that he had made "a real American pioneer journey into the wilderness behind an ox team hitched to a farm wagon." Despite storms and mosquitoes, he asserted that he was "in the best of health." His letters, published in* Nordisk Folkeblad, *led to his appointment as an agent of the Minnesota State Board of Immigration. Hjelm-Hansen died in Goodhue County in 1880.*

August 11, 1869

We passed through Chippewa Station and Evansville [Douglas County], where the stage changed horses, and where there are stores. At the latter place, which is surrounded by Norwegian and Swedish settlements, Mr. Lewiston has lately established himself in business, and Dr. Rasch in-tends to settle here also. From the height on which Evansville is located, there is a wide and lovely view of fruitful prairies, beautiful patches of wood and small lakes. All the land hereabouts is either taken by settlers or is in the hands of speculators. About 4 miles north of Evansville, the road passes the northern corner of Pelican Lake, which is the most beau-tiful spot I have seen on the journey. The lake is quite large, being about 8 miles long and 6 miles wide, and is connected by a smalt strade [narrow strait] with Lake Christina, which is about of equal size. From the lake, the land rises like an amphitheater. The choicest farming country alter-nates with lovely patches of wood, and in the lake, small forest clad is-lands lift themselves out of the water.

This marvelous country lay open to homesteading until 2 years ago. Now it is occupied by Norsemen and Swedes, among whom are a large number of bachelors, some of whom possibly intend to sell their homestead rights or rather their labor when good opportunities offer. At the northern end of Pelican Lake begins the great uninhabited prairie which stretches all the way to Fort Garry in the territory of the English. About halfway between Pelican Lake and Pomme de Terre Station is a pretty little lake surrounded by forest. At this place two Norsemen have taken homesteads just this year. From Pomme de Terre to Fort Abercrombie the prairie is like a green sea, the tall grass resembling the billows. To the eastward one may see the bare earth here and there, but to the westward in the great Otter Tail country the eye sees nothing save the green sea of grass....

The whole prairie, which is perfectly level, is the best land one could desire. The soil is a rich loam mixed with a little sand upon an underlayer of clay. On this prairie there is room for thousands of farmers. The woods consist chiefly of elm, ash, and oak....

On the evening of the sixth day we reached Georgetown, which lies about 50 miles North of Fort Abercrombie at the juncture of the Red and the Buffalo rivers. At this place a beginning has been made in laying out a town.... The location of Georgetown makes it almost certain that in the near future it will be a busy and thriving town. It is the natural center of a very large and fruitful territory, both in Minnesota and Dakota, a region to which settlers will rush in large numbers as soon as the railroad is finished....

With reference to the question of settling, it is my opinion, as well as the opinion of every man who has seen this country, that it offers so many advantages for Scandinavian farmers that it may be taken for granted that immigrants will stream into this region in the near future. Doubtless within 10 years the whole country will be settled and under cultivation, and it will then be one of the most beautiful and fruitful sections of America. The soil is of the richest sort and easily cultivated, for there is neither stone nor stump to bother the plow. There is sufficient timber to be had along the rivers, and the railroads will run through the center of the valley. Already there is steamboat service from the British possessions to Georgetown, and within a few years these will undoubtedly ascend much further.

The profits on agricultural products sold to the forts and to the Hudson Bay Co. should be handsome. The water power in both rivers—the Red and the Buffalo—should be sufficient for all kinds of factories, and the climate is very healthful. During the summer months, May, June, July, and August, the heat is at times oppressive, but there is usually a refreshing breeze. During September and October the weather is as a rule very pleasant. November brings winter which lasts until the middle of March with a temperature very like that of western Norway. During the winter the snow covers the prairie to a depth of two or three feet, and roads may be made wherever desired. The spring work begins in the latter part of March or during the first part of April and harvest begins in July or August. As I contemplate this region, I am conscious of a wish that many of my country men (the Scandinavians) would come up here to settle the land lying between Fort Abercrombie and Georgetown, and especially along the rivers on either side of the peninsular prairie. Each man may get a 160 acre homestead, and if he is in position to do so, he may buy an additional 160 for $200. With a 320 acre farm of such soil, every family which does not make too great demands should make a good living. I am myself willing to settle here if, as I hope, there may even this fall be made a settlement of at least 50 such neighbors as I desire, who would be willing to build a church and a school immediately. My fellow travelers, Messrs. Brown and Torgersen, and other able men are also prepared to do likewise. To the North of Georgetown are splendid opportunities for those who wish to engage in stock breeding or ranching. In this connection, it should be said that parts of this region during very wet seasons is subject to floods. However during the past 20 years, I am told, there has been only one such flood, and that was two years ago when other parts of Minnesota also suffered. But should a man refrain from settling in places which are subject to such natural catastrophes, the largest and most fruitful parts of the earth would be uninhabited. . . .

I have reason to believe that a company of honorable men will be formed here in Alexandria with a view to lead such Scandinavian families who wish to go to the Red River Valley. Such families as desire further information may apply to this company. . . .

On my return to Alexandria, I was pleasurably surprised to meet the Rev. Brandt from Decora[h]. He uses his vacations in traveling about in the Norwegian settlements of this region to conduct services among the people. He baptizes, confirms, administers the sacrament, and preaches. Immediately after his arrival, to the great joy and edification of the Scandinavian people, he conducted a service in the beautiful little Methodist church in the town. The next day he proceeded to the neighborhood of Pelican Lake. Today he is to be present at a large meeting of Norwegian farmers near Holmes City, where a subscription is to be taken to buy a parsonage and to raise the salary of a resident pastor. Among these farmers are many serious minded Christians, who feel sorely the lack of regular services and the preaching of God's word. These men are glad to give of their means in order to supply this lack as soon as possible.

I have received an inquiry from a Dane in Milwaukee and from the head of a family here in Alexandria whether a girl of over 21 years could take a homestead. They had been told that only girls with children might take a homestead. How such an idea could have come into the minds of the people that the wise men who framed the homestead law would encourage and reward immorality in such a "eklatant" manner, I do not understand nor does it matter. Be that as it may it is not the case. Any girl or widow 21 years of age has the same rights and privileges as a man to take a homestead. There may be cases in which a girl or a widow may desire to make use of this privilege, and therefore it is well that they had correct information in the matter. I have myself seen two sisters in Wisconsin who are operating a good sized farm without hiring much male help. As land-owners, bachelor ladies could assure themselves of independence and a living by renting or taking a share man. . . .

Farewell I am going about to set out for the Great Otter Tail County, where during the past two years so many Scandinavians have settled.

Nordisk Folkebladet (Minneapolis), Aug. 11, 1869, Sigurd Melby, trans., Paul Hjelm-Hansen Papers, MHS.

For Further Reading

Blegen, Theodore C. *Norwegian Migration to America.* 2 vols. Northfield: Norwegian-American Historical Assn., 1931–40.

Gjerde, Jon. *The Minds of the West: Ethnocultural Evolution in the Rural Middle West, 1830–1917.* Chapel Hill: University of North Carolina Press, 1997.

Holmquist, June D., ed. *They Chose Minnesota: A Survey of the State's Ethnic Groups.* St. Paul: Minnesota Historical Society Press, 1981.

Lovoll, Odd S. *The Promise of America: A History of the Norwegian-American People.* Minneapolis: University of Minnesota Press, 1984.

————. *The Promise Fulfilled: A Portrait of Norwegian Americans Today.* Minneapolis: University of Minnesota Press, in cooperation with the Norwegian-American Historical Assn., 1998.

Nelson, Marion, ed. *Norwegian Folk Art: The Migration of a Tradition.* New York: Abbeville Press, 1995.

Øverland, Orm. *The Western Home: A Literary History of Norwegian America.* Northfield: Norwegian-American Historical Assn., 1996.

————. *Immigrant Minds, American Identities: Making the United States Home, 1870–1930.* Urbana: University of Illinois Press, 2000.

Semmingsen, Ingrid. *Norway to America: A History of the Migration.* Translated by Einar Haugen. Minneapolis: University of Minnesota Press, 1978.

Stokker, Kathleen. *Keeping Christmas: Yuletide Traditions in Norway and the New Land.* St. Paul: Minnesota Historical Society Press, 2000.

Notes

1. Carl G. O. Hansen, *My Minneapolis: A Chronicle of What Has Been Learned and Observed About the Norwegians in Minneapolis Through One Hundred Years,* 11 (Minneapolis, 1956). The authors wish to acknowledge the helpful suggestions received during their work on this book from Professors Odd S. Lovoll, Carl H. Chrislock, and David Mauk.

2. Arlow W. Andersen, *The Norwegian-Americans* 38 (Boston, 1975); United States, *Census,* 1910, *Population,* 2:991; 1970, vol. 1, part 25, pp. 12–15, 514, *Census,* 1990, *Social and Economic Characteristics: Minnesota,* 67, 205–13; State of Minnesota, *Census, 1905,* 195; Odd Lovoll, *The Promise Fulfilled: A Portrait of Norwegian Americans Today,* 47–51 (Minneapolis, 1998). Categories shift from one decennial census to the next. In some census calculations, Norwegians were counted with Swedes. The foreign-stock figures are too inconsistently presented to give a definitive picture of the changing numbers of native-born persons with Norway-born parents. In 1980, when one could give only one ancestry, only 267,853 Minnesotans considered themselves of Norwegian background. When people could state multiple ancestries in 1990, the number was considerably larger. According to a count of listings in 2001 telephone directories for Minneapolis and St. Paul, the National Football League team and 79 businesses in the Twin Cities alone carried the name Viking.

3. Theodore C. Blegen, *Norwegian Migration to America, 1825–1860,* 22 (Northfield, 1931), hereafter cited as vol. 1; Ingrid Semmingsen, *Norway to America: A History of the Migration,* 100–102 (Minneapolis, 1978); Semmingsen, "The Dissolution of Estate Society in Norway," in *Scandinavian Economic History Review,* 2:[166]–203 (1954); Michael Drake, *Population and Society in Norway, 1735–1865* (Cambridge, Eng., 1969). For a more recent view of the Norwegian society that produced the emigrants, see Francis Sejersted, *Den Vanskelige Frihet, 1814–51,* especially 97, 103–9, 120–25 (*Norges Historie,* vol. 10 – Oslo, 1978).

The traditional explanation of a falling death rate linked to the introduction of the potato and the increasing use of vaccines against smallpox has been questioned by recent research. See Kåre Lunden, "Potetdyrkinga og den raskare folketalsvoksteren i Noreg frå 1815," in *Historisk tidsskrift,* 54:4, p. 275–313, English summary, 313–15 (1975); Edgar Hovland et al., "Poteta og folkeveksten i Noreg etter 1815: Fire debattinnlegg," in *Historisk tidsskrift,* 57:3, p. 251–99 (1978).

4. It is debatable whether the new machinery pushed laborers off the land or the decline in the labor pool forced farmers to mechanize. Recent research suggests the latter, since mechanization occurred later than the rural emigration and in regions where emigration was less pronounced. See Semmingsen, *Norway to America,* 104, 108–10, and Kjell Haarstad, "Utvandrerne fra bygdene – presset eller lokket," in Arnfinn Engen et al., *Utvandringa – det store oppbrotet,* 38–56 (Oslo, 1978), for differing interpretations.

5. Semmingsen, *Norway to America,*

34–36, 40: Peter A. Munch, *A Study of Cultural Change: Rural-Urban Conflicts in Norway*, 41–46, 52, 59 (*Studia Norvegica: Ethnologica and Folkloristica*, no. 9 — Oslo, 1956).

6. Ingrid Semmingsen, "Origin of Nordic Emigration," in *American Studies in Scandinavia*, 9:14 (1977); Andersen, *Norwegian-Americans*, 4, 59–71. Nicholas Tavuchis, *Pastors and Immigrants: The Role of a Religious Elite in the Absorption of Norwegian Immigrants*, 13–21 (The Hague, 1963), estimated that seven out of eight immigrants left from rural districts in the early stages of immigration up to 1865. See also George T. Flom, *A History of Norwegian Immigration to the United States from the Earliest Beginning down to the Year 1848*, 33 (Iowa City, Ia., 1909).

7. Carlton C. Qualey, *Norwegian Settlement in the United States*, 17–75, 112 (Reprint ed., New York, 1970); Ingrid Semmingsen, *Veien Mot Vest: Utvandringen Fra Norge, 1865–1915*, 2:74 (Oslo, 1950); Semmingsen, "Emigration and the Image of America in Europe," in Henry S. Commager, ed., *Immigration and American History: Essays in Honor of Theodore C. Blegen*, 26–54 (Minneapolis, 1961). For a complete translation of the letter below, see Carlton C. Qualey, trans. and ed., "Three America Letters to Lesja," in *Norwegian-American Studies*, 27:46–48 (Northfield, 1977); for a collection of these letters in English, see Theodore C. Blegen, *Land of Their Choice: The Immigrants Write Home* (Minneapolis, 1955).

8. Here and below, on origins of the earliest emigrants and the geographical development of the migration itself, see Flom, *Norwegian Immigration*, 376–79; Semmingsen, *Norway to America*, 33; Semmingsen, *Veien Mot Vest*, 2:493;

Theodore C. Blegen, *Norwegian Migration to America: The American Transition*, 74–77 (Northfield, 1940), hereafter cited as vol. 2; Odd S. Lovoll, *A Folk Epic: The Bygdelag in America*, 8–10 (Boston, 1975); Hjalmar R. Holand, *Norwegians in America: The Last Migration*, 31–40 (Sioux Falls, S.Dak., 1978), an English translation by Helmer M. Blegen of Holand's *Den Siste Folkevandring* published in Norwegian in 1930. The latter is a selective condensation with some additions of Holand's longer study, *De Norske Settlementers Historie* (Ephraim, Wis., 1909). An excellent series of maps showing the districts in all the Nordic countries from which emigrants left during five-year periods between 1865 and 1914 is in Harald Runblom and Hans Norman, eds., *From Sweden to America: A History of the Migration*, between pp. 128 and 129 (Stockholm and Minneapolis, 1976).

9. For detailed discussions of Norwegian settlement in southeastern Minnesota, see Qualey, *Norwegian Settlement*, 97–119; Holand, *De Norske Settlementers Historie*, 358–501. For a case study of the "chain migration" among Norwegian immigrants, see Jon Gjerde, "Chain Migration: A Case Study from Western Norway," in Rudolph J. Vecoli and Suzanne M. Sinke, eds., *A Century of European Migrations, 1830–1930*, 158–81 (Champaign, Ill., 1991).

10. *Billed-Magazin* (Madison, Wis.), August 1869, p. 287, quoted in Theodore L. Nydahl, "The Early Norwegian Settlement of Goodhue County, Minnesota," 16, master's thesis, University of Minnesota, 1929; Semmingsen, *Veien Mot Vest*, 2:54, 57.

11. Here and below, see Carlton C. Qualey, "A Typical Norwegian Settlement: Spring Grove, Minnesota," in *Norwegian-*

American Studies, 9:54–66 (Northfield, 1936); Ole S. Johnson, Nybyggerhistorie fra Spring Grove og omegn Minnesota, 103, 123 (Minneapolis, 1920); Plat Book of Houston County, Minnesota, 6 (Philadelphia, 1878); Franklyn Curtiss-Wedge, ed., History of Houston County Minnesota, 173–81 (Winona, 1919); U.S. manuscript census schedules, 1870, Houston County, Spring Grove, roll 6, microfilm in MHS; Einar Haugen, The Norwegian Language in America: A Study in Bilingual Behavior, 2:337–60 (Philadelphia, 1953). Mixtures of Norwegian dialects in Minnesota settlements produced identifiable American Norwegian ones such as the "Spring Grove dialect"; Haugen, 2:351. On the church, see Sydney L. Roppe and Blayne Onsgard, History of Spring Grove, [15–19] (Spring Grove, 1952).

12. Jon A. Gjerde, "The Effect of Community on Migration: Three Minnesota Townships," in Journal of Historical Geography, 5:403–22 (October 1979); Peter A. Munch, ed., The Strange American Way: Letters of Caja Munch from Wiota Wisconsin, 1855–1859, 118 (Carbondale, Ill., 1970). In one year, for example, members of the North Prairie Lutheran Church in Arendahl Township, Fillmore County, gave $762.50 toward the construction of a church erected 10 years after the first Norwegian settlers arrived. A year later in 1864, still heavily in debt, the congregation contributed $609 toward the building of Luther College of Decorah, Ia. See North Prairie Lutheran Church, Eightieth Anniversary Year Book: A Brief Historical Sketch, 7–9 (Minneapolis, [1936]).

13. J. S. J[ohnson], Valdris Helsing, 7:80 (May, 1905), quoted in Haugen, Norwegian Language in America, 1:34; Telesoga, 33:30 (September, 1917), quoted in Lovoll,

A Folk Epic, 13. On the Norwegian Lutheran church, see p. 31, below.

14. Statistics derived from a sampling of Det statistiske Sentralbyrå records, quoted in Semmingsen, Veien Mot Vest, 2:492; U.S. manuscript census schedules, 1870, Houston County, Spring Grove, roll 6; U.S., Census, 1870, Population, 606. Of the children born outside of Minnesota, 76.7% were born in Norway. Minnesota's foreign born as a whole had a ratio of 127.7 to 100 in 1870. Norwegian migration was more family centered than that of the British Isles and Ireland in which only 19% were children under 12.

15. Jon Gjerde and Anne C. McCants, "Individual Life Chances within the Rural Family, 1850–1910: A Norwegian-American Example," Journal of Interdisciplinary History 30 (1999): 377–405; Amerika (Chicago), July 29, 1885, quoted in Qualey, Norwegian Settlements, 12.

16. Qualey, Norwegian Settlements, 124–126; Holand, De Norske Settlementers Historie, 533. The Linden settlement occupied portions of southern Brown and western Blue Earth Counties as well as most of Watonwan County. The Park Region is here defined as Becker, Otter Tail, Pope, Kandiyohi, Douglas, Swift, Todd, western Stearns and Meeker, and eastern Grant and Stevens Counties.

17. Holand, De Norske Settlementers Historie, 485, 509; Stageberg and Flaten, both quoted in Nydahl, "Early Norwegian Settlement of Goodhue County," 36, 37. Minnesota county histories provide impressionistic views of these strung-out communities. The earliest settlers in Freeborn, Kandiyohi, and Martin Counties were largely from Rock Prairie. In Lincoln County, the Spring Grove settlement served as the mother colony. The earliest

Redwood County Norwegian had lived in Fillmore County. The pattern suggests numerous parallel, northwesterly movements frequently with little contact among them in spite of the similarity of direction.

18. [Gena Lee Gilbertson], *Big Grove Norwegian Lutheran Church 75th Anniversary, 1867–1942*, 6–10, 80–89 (Grand Forks, N.Dak., 1942); Big Grove Norwegian Lutheran Church Records, microfilm roll 306, American Lutheran Church Archives, Dubuque, Ia., calculations in Minnesota Ethnic History Project (MEHP) Papers, Minnesota Historical Society (MHS). The actual figure was 69.1%. Because of its Halling background, Big Grove in 1911 was the site of a three-day convention of some 6,000 Halling-Americans who gathered from throughout the U.S.; Lovoll, *A Folk Epic*, 90.

19. Qualey, *Norwegian Settlements*, 120.

20. Taped interview of Johanna Nelson Aune and Gertie Nelson Holm, April 9, 1976, who grew up in Spring Prairie Township, Clay County, one of an extensive collection of oral history interviews of Red River Valley Scandinavians in Northwest Minnesota Historical Center, Moorhead; Peter A. Munch, "History and Sociology," in *Norwegian-American Studies*, 20:53 (Northfield, 1959). See also note 43, below.

21. Qualey, *Norwegian Settlements*, 120.

22. Lars Ljungmark, *For Sale—Minnesota: Organized Promotion of Scandinavian Immigration, 1866–1873*, 61 (Chicago, 1971). For more on Hjelm-Hansen, see Personal Account, p. 77.

23. *Nordisk Folkeblad* (Minneapolis), Aug. 11, 1869; Ljungmark, *For Sale—Minnesota*, 62–64: Qualey, *Norwegian Settlements*, 127.

24. Levi Thortvedt, "The Early History of the Red River Valley," 1–11, 29, 35, in Levi Thortvedt Papers, MHS. See also Dora J. Gunderson, "The Settlement of Clay County, Minnesota, 1870–1900," 27–30, master's thesis, University of Minnesota, 1929; *Clay County Land Atlas & Plat Book*, 32 (Rockford, Ill., 1976).

25. Thortvedt, "History," 36; calculated from Minnesota, *Census, 1875*, table facing p. 98, and *1905*, 134, 156, 163, 168–70; Gunderson, "Settlement of Clay County," 59.

26. Martin Ulvestad, *Nordmændene i Amerika, deres Historie og Rekord*, 1:87, 90, 95, 102, 107, 112–14, 117–19, 121, 123 (Minneapolis, 1907); Mrs. Gerald Olson and Mrs. Joel W. Johnson, eds., *In the Heart of the Red River Valley: A History of the People of Norman County, Minnesota*, 2 ([Ada?], 1976); Hazel H. Wahlberg, *The North Land: A History of Roseau County*, 115, 126 (Roseau, 1975); *Pioneer Tales: A History of Pennington County*, 499 (Thief River Falls, 1976); interview of Hazel H. Wahlberg by Deborah Stultz, May 21, 1980, notes in MEHP Papers. Other county and local histories of the Red River Valley and elsewhere contain much information about Norwegian-American activities and organizations in rural and small-town Minnesota. See, for example, Roberta Olson, *Fertile—Hub of the Sand Hill Valley*, 11, 67 ([Fertile, 1975?]) on Polk County, and Blanche Iverson, *Buzzle Township, Pinewood, Minnesota, 1898–1976* (Pinewood, 1976) on Beltrami County.

27. Nicolay A. Grevstad, "The Norwegians in America," in Martin Ulvestad, *Norsk-Amerikaneren Vikingesaga samt Pioneerhistorie, statistik og biografiske Oplysninger om Nordmænd i Amerika*, 215, 216 (Seattle, 1928); U.S., *Census*, 1909–10, *Agriculture*, 5:181; Torger A. Hoverstad, *The Norwegian Farmers in the United*

States, 7, 11–13 (Fargo, N.Dak., 1915); Andersen, *Norwegian-Americans,* 87.

28. Odd S. Lovoll and Kenneth O. Bjork, *The Norwegian-American Historical Association, 1925–1975,* 2 (Northfield, 1975); Stanley S. Guterman, "The Americanization of Norwegian Immigrants: A Study in Historical Sociology," in *Sociology and Social Research,* 52:252–70 (April, 1968); Hoverstad, *Norwegian Farmers,* 11; Aftenposten, *Facts about Norway,* 6 (Oslo, 1977); *Folkebladet,* May 5, 1886; Gunderson, "The Settlement of Clay County," 62. On the other hand, a study of population changes in Stevens County showed a decline of Norwegians in both the village of Morris and in Morris Township from 1885 to 1895; see Peggy Cottrell, "Immigration in Stevens County, 1870–1890," tables 2, 3, course paper, 1973, in West Central Minnesota Historical Center, Morris, copy in MEHP Papers.

29. Semmingsen, *Veien Mot Vest,* 2:246; Matti Kaups, "Norwegian Immigrants and the Development of Commercial Fisheries along the North Shore of Lake Superior: 1870–1895," in Harald S. Naess, ed., *Norwegian Influence on the Upper Midwest,* 21–34 (Duluth, 1976). Both the MHS and the Northeast Minnesota Historical Center in Duluth have excellent collections of taped and transcribed oral history interviews with North Shore fishermen, including a number of Norwegians. The Norwegians on the range were largely from the southeastern regions of Akershus and Buskerud and the west coast from Bergen to Nordland. Although appreciable numbers worked in mining, they were not nearly as numerous as the Swedes. John Sirjamaki, "The People of the Mesabi Range," in *Minnesota History,* 27:206–10, 212 (September 1946).

30. Semmingsen, *Norway to America,* 112–15; Lennart Jörberg, "The Industrial Revolution in the Nordic Countries," in Carlo M. Cipolla, ed., *The Emergence of Industrial Societies,* 377–80, 453 (*The Fontana Economic History of Europe,* vol. 4, part 2—Reprint ed., New York, 1976); Ingrid Semmingsen, "Family Emigration from Bergen 1874–92," in Harald S. Naess and Sigmund Skard, eds., *Americana Norvegica: Studies in Scandinavian-American Interrelations Dedicated to Einar Haugen,* 3:38–63 (Oslo, 1971); Semmingsen, *Veien Mot Vest,* 460–70. Semmingsen saw the Norwegian city as a "stage" in the move to America. She also found that of the nearly 50,000 remigrants in Norway in 1920, many who had been industrial workers and miners in the U.S. returned to take up farming; 82% of the men returned to their home communities. On urban emigration from Norway, see Peter Rinnan and Rolf Kåre Østrem, "Utvandringen fra Kristiania 1880–1907. en studie i urbanutvandring," master's thesis, University of Oslo, 1979.

31. Lincoln Steffens, *The Shame of the Cities,* 64 (New York, 1904).

32. David Mauk provided the author with information from his study of Norwegians in the Twin Cities. The general data were extracted from U.S., *Census,* 1880, *Population,* 451; 1890, part 1, p. 2, 370.

33. John S. Johnson, *Minnesota, En Kortfattet Historie av Nordmændenes Bebyggelse av Staten,* 160 (St. Paul, 1914); Hansen, *My Minneapolis,* 52–54. The Norwegians lived with some Danes and more Swedes in Minneapolis' West Bank and South Side neighborhoods; see June Drenning Holmquist, ed., *They Chose Minnesota: A Survey of the State's Ethnic Groups* (St. Paul, 1981), Chapters 12 and 13.

34. Hansen, *My Minneapolis*, 145–52. See also Dan Armitage, "The Curling Waters: A West Bank History," in *Minnesota Daily* (Minneapolis), Sept. 27, 1973, p. 15–25. Here and below, see Calvin F. Schmid, *Social Saga of Two Cities: An Ecological and Statistical Study*, 157–60 (Minneapolis, 1937). Norwegians were far less numerous in St. Paul; see Schmid, 135, 155.

35. Information from David Mauk, who was undertaking a study of Norwegians in the Twin Cities.

36. For an elaboration of rural-urban differences, see Guterman, in *Sociology and Social Research*, 52:252–70; Hansen, *My Minneapolis*, 29, 54, 63–92. A similar cooperative situation existed in the Scandinavian community of Duluth, where the 1870 census counted 625 Swedes and 242 Norwegians. *Det Nordiske Forbund* was founded there in 1871 for social and other purposes, and the community supported *Duluth Skandinav*, a newspaper established in 1887 that lasted for 78 years. Jørgen Fuhr edited and later published the paper from 1915 until his death in 1930; Anna, his widow, then ran the Fuhr Publishing and Printing Co. for 25 years until illness forced her to sell in 1955. *Duluth City Directory*, 1915, 1930, 1958; *Duluth News-Tribune*, Nov. 24, 1956, p. 6; Matti Kaups, "Europeans in Duluth: 1870," in Ryck Lydecker and Lawrence J. Sommer, eds., *Duluth: Sketches of the Past*, 74, 78 (Duluth, 1976).

37. Hansen, *My Minneapolis*, 114, 118, 128. On Norwegian American workers, see John R. Jensvold, "In Search of a Norwegian-American Working Class," in *Minnesota History*, 50: 63–70 (Summer 1986).

38. Nina Draxten, *Kristofer Janson in America*, 100, 197, 218 (Boston, 1976); Carl H. Chrislock, *From Fjord to Freeway: 100 Years, Augsburg College*, 43 (Minneapolis, 1969); Gerald Thorson, "Tinsel and Dust: Disenchantment in Two Minneapolis Novels from the 1880s," in *Minnesota History*, 45:210–22 (Summer 1977); Hansen, *My Minneapolis*, 99–109; Arthur C. Paulson, "Bjørnson and the Norwegian-Americans," in *Norwegian-American Studies*, 5:84–109 (Northfield, 1930). The Nora Free Christian Church, founded by Janson at Hanska, Brown County, continued as the Nora Unitarian Universalist Church in 2001; the Unitarian church at Underwood, Otter Tail County, which he organized as the Underwood Free Christian Church, endured as a Unitarian Universalist church; the Nazareth Church in Minneapolis persisted only until 1906; Draxten, 56, 330; interview of Pastor Paul Johnson of the Nora Church by Deborah Stultz, May 12, 1980, notes in MEHP Papers. For more on Bjørnson in the U.S., see Eva L. Haugen and Einar Haugen, eds. and trans., *Land of the Free: Bjørnstjerne Bjørnson's America Letters, 1880–1881* (Northfield, 1978).

39. Chrislock, *From Fjord to Freeway*, 33; Carl H. Chrislock to Deborah Stultz, Dec. 27, 1980, in MEHP Papers.

40. Todd Nichol, "Temples Made With Hands: A Norwegian-American Lutheran Congregation and Its Houses of Worship," in *Lutheran Quarterly*, 11:423–62 (Winter 1997). See also James S. Hamre, *From Immigrant Parish to Inner City Ministry: Trinity Lutheran Congregation, 1868–1998* (N.p., 1998).

41. Carl G. O. Hansen, *History of Sons of Norway*, 13–16 (Minneapolis, 1944).

42. Hansen, *History of Sons of Norway*, 32; C. Sverre Norborg, *An American Saga*, 52 (Minneapolis, 1970); Lovoll, *A Folk Epic*, 22.

43. Waldemar Ager, "Norsk-amerikansk skjønliteratur," in Johs. B. Wist, ed., *Norsk-Amerikanernes Festskrift 1914,* 294 (Decorah, Ia., 1914); Todd W. Nichol, ed. and trans., *Vivacious Daughter: Seven Lectures on the Religious Situation among Norwegians in America by Herman Amberg Preus,* 34 (Northfield, 1990); Semmingsen, *Norway to America,* 83.

44. E. Clifford Nelson and Eugene L. Fevold, *The Lutheran Church among Norwegian-Americans: A History of the Evangelical Lutheran Church,* 1:123–25 (Minneapolis, 1960). Some Norwegians did join Methodist and Baptist churches, often in association with Danes. On the Methodists, see Arlow W. Andersen, *The Salt of the Earth: A History of Norwegian-Danish Methodism in America* (Nashville, 1962); on the Baptists, see P. Stiansen, *History of the Norwegian Baptists in America* (Wheaton, Ill., 1939). The records of some Minnesota Norwegian Lutheran churches are available in MHS; see, for example, entries 2427, 2593, 2708 in Lydia A. Lucas, comp., *Manuscripts Collections of the Minnesota Historical Society, Guide Number 3* (St. Paul, 1977).

45. Hansen, *My Minneapolis,* 94; Nelson and Fevold, *Lutheran Church among Norwegian-Americans,* 2:4, 222, 305. Election is doctrinally similar to Calvinist predestination; for particulars, see Nelson and Fevold, 1:254. U. V. Koren, "Hvad den Norske Synods har villet og fremdeles vil," *Samlede Skrifter* 3:444 (1890); Jon Gjerde, *The Minds of the West: The Ethnocultural Evolution in the Rural Middle West, 1830–1917,* 112–29 (Chapel Hill, 1997). Minnesota figures were calculated from O. M. Norlie, *Norsk Lutherske Menigheter i Amerika, 1843–1916,* 436–840 (Minneapolis, 1918).

46. Here and below, see Blegen, *Norwegian Migration to America,* 2:518, 530; Merrill E. Jarchow, *Private Liberal Arts Colleges in Minnesota: Their History and Contributions,* 25–33, 41–43, 77–88, 101–5, 185–99, 216–23 (St. Paul, 1973); Joseph M. Shaw, *Bernt Julius Muus: Founder of St. Olaf College* (Northfield, 1999); Norlie, *Norsk Lutherske Menigheter,* 1:835; Andersen, *Norwegian-Americans,* 104, 130; Hansen, *My Minneapolis,* 302–18. It is interesting to note that Muskego Church, the first in the U.S. built by Norwegian immigrants in 1843–44, was moved from Wisconsin to the campus of Luther Seminary in 1904. It may still be seen there. Sue E. Holbert and June D. Holmquist, *A History Tour of 50 Twin City Landmarks,* 24 (St. Paul, 1966).

47. Neil T. Eckstein, "The Social Criticism of Ole Edvart Rølvaag," in *Norwegian-American Studies,* 24:122 (Northfield, 1970).

48. Blegen, *Norwegian Migration to America,* 2:281, 284, 289, 547; Semmingsen, *Norway to America,* 138; Arlow W. Andersen, *The Immigrant Takes His Stand: The Norwegian-American Press and Public Affairs, 1847–1872,* 12 (Northfield, 1953).

49. This paragraph and the one that follows were based on information compiled by the MHS Newspaper Department and on John A. Fagereng, "Norwegian Social and Cultural Life in Minnesota, 1868–1891: An Analysis of Typical Norwegian Newspapers," 1–11, master's thesis, University of Minnesota, 1932; interview of Jenny A. Johnson, editor of *Minnesota Posten,* by Deborah Stultz, May 22, 1980, notes in MEHP Papers. Many of the papers were printed in Norwegian, Danish, and/or English. For more on the Norwegian press in Minnesota, see Carl

Hansen and Johs. B. Wist, "Den Norsk-Amerikanske Presse," in Wist, ed., *Norsk-Amerikanernes Festskrift*, 9–203.

50. Richard B. Eide, comp., *Norse Immigrant Letters: Glimpses of Norse Immigrant Life in the Northwest in the Fifties*, 6 (Minneapolis, 1925); Orm Øverland, *The Western Home: A Literary History of Norwegian America*, 33 (Northfield, 1996); Blegen, *Norwegian Migration to America*, 2:327; Fagereng, "Norwegian Social and Cultural Life," 18, 43.

51. On the content of various papers, see Fagereng, "Norwegian Social and Cultural Life," 16, 25, 62–97, 107–11, 114. 121–23; Wist, ed., *Norsk-Amerikanernes Festskrift*, 105, 119.

52. Jon Wefald, *A Voice of Protest: Norwegians in American Politics, 1890–1917*, 32–44 (Northfield, 1971); *Gaa Paa!*, December 6, 1917, p. 1; Odd S. Lovoll, "*Gaa Paa:* A Scandinavian Voice of Dissent," in *Minnesota History*, 52:86–99 (Fall 1990).

53. The other statue depicts Swedish-born John A. Johnson. See George H. Mayer, *The Political Career of Floyd B. Olson*, 171 (Minneapolis, 1951). On Nelson's career, see Walter B. Evans, "The Early Political Career of Knute Nelson, 1867–1892," master's thesis, University of Minnesota, 1937; Millard L. Gieske, "The Politics of Knute Nelson, 1912–1920," Ph.D. thesis, University of Minnesota, 1965; Gieske and Steven J. Keillor, *Norwegian Yankee: Knute Nelson and the Failure of American Politics, 1860–1923* (Northfield, 1995).

54. Wefald, *Voice of Protest*, 4–7, 18–24, 30; Andersen, *Norwegian-Americans*, 4–8. No thorough investigations have been made, however, of the class backgrounds of Norwegian Americans active in politics in Minnesota or elsewhere.

55. Wefald, *Voice of Protest*, 24.

56. Here and below, see Laurence M. Larson, *The Changing West and Other Essays*, 76–78 (Northfield, 1937); Carl H. Chrislock, "The Norwegian-American Impact on Minnesota Politics: How Far 'Left-of-Center'?" in Naess, ed., *Norwegian Influence on the Upper Midwest*, 106–8, 111–16; Sten Carlsson, "Scandinavian Politicians in Minnesota Around the Turn of the Century," in Naess and Skard, eds., *Americana Norvegica*, 3:263–67; Gieske and Keillor, *Norwegian Yankee: Knute Nelson*, 97–119. On the economic status of Norwegian wheat farmers in the Red River Valley, see Charles R. Lamb, "Up from the Wheat Fields: The Nonpartisan League's Expansion into Minnesota," 48, 49, Plan B paper, University of Minnesota, 1979, copy in MHS. Norwegians constituted 28.4% of the four ethnic groups, yet in 1893 there were 12 Norwegians compared to 12 of German, Swedish, and Danish birth or parentage; in 1901 there were 17 and 16; in 1917, 21 and 22; and in 1931, 30 compared to 28; Wefald, *Voice of Protest*, 24, 27.

57. J. J. Skordalsvold editorial in *Heimdal* (St. Paul) and John M. Hetland letter to the editor, *Norman County Herald* (Ada), April 11, 1890, both quoted in Wefald, *Voice of Protest*, 47. Owen carried 24 Minnesota counties; Wefald, 47–52. See also Carl H. Chrislock, "The Politics of Protest in Minnesota, 1890–1901: From Populism to Progressivism," Ph.D. thesis, University of Minnesota, 1954.

58. H. G. Stordock to Knute Nelson, March 19, 1892, in Knute Nelson Papers, MHS, quoted in Wefald, *Voice of Protest*, 49. This prediction proved true for Polk and Otter Tail Counties; see Wefald, 47, 51. See also Gieske and Keillor, *Norwegian Yankee: Knute Nelson*, 145–98.

59. Chrislock, in Naess, ed., *Norwegian Influence*, 109, quoting Michael Barone, "The Social Basis of Urban Politics: Minneapolis and St. Paul, 1890–1905," honors paper, Harvard University, 1965.

60. Lowell J. Soike, *Norwegian Americans and the Politics of Dissent, 1880–1924* (Northfield, 1991).

61. Chrislock, in Naess, ed., *Norwegian Influence*, 114; Bruce M. White *et al.*, comps., *Minnesota Votes: Election Returns by County for Presidents, Senators, Congressmen, and Governors, 1857–1977*, 220, 224 (St. Paul, 1977); James M. Shields, *Mr. Progressive: A Biography of Elmer Austin Benson*, 14 (Minneapolis, 1971); Mayer, *Floyd B. Olson*, 7–9. On the Nonpartisan League and ethnic groups, see Lamb, "Up from the Wheat Fields," 45, 46.

62. Wefald most successfully presented this point of view in *Voice of Protest*, 34–44, 55–72, but failed to examine the Norwegian Republican elements in the southeast.

63. *Star Tribune* (Minneapolis), June 21, 2001, p. 1A, 13A; Sten Carlsson, "Scandinavian Politicians in Minnesota around the Turn of the Century: A Study of the Role of the Ethnic Factor in an Immigrant State," in Harald S. Naess and Sigmund Skard, eds., *Americana Norvegica*, 3:263–67 (1971), cited in Lovoll, *The Promise Fulfilled*, 109. Lieutenant governor Hjalmar Petersen, of Danish descent, became governor in 1936 on the death of Floyd B. Olson, but he was never elected to that office in his own right.

64. Ager, in Wist, ed., *Norsk-Amerikanernes Festskrift*, 294; Orm Øverland, *The Western Home*.

65. Laurence M. Larson, "Tellef Grundysen and the Beginnings of Norwegian-American Fiction," in *Norwegian-American Studies*, 8:6 (Northfield, 1934); Dorothy B. Skårdal, *The Divided Heart: Scandinavian Immigrant Experience through Literary Sources*, 35–38 (Oslo, 1974); Ager, in Wist, ed., *Norsk-Amerikanernes Festskrift*, 296; Odd G. Andreassen, "Lars Andreas Stenholt: Norwegian-American Author," 1, 11–31, thesis paper, University of Oslo, 1977, copy in MHS; Andersen, *Norwegian-Americans*, 174; Semmingsen, *Norway to America*, 140–42; Harald Naess, "Ygdrasil Literary Society, 1896–1971," in Brita Seyersted, ed., *Americana Norvegica: Norwegian Contributions to American Studies Dedicated to Sigmund Skard*, 4:31–45 (Oslo, 1973). Aftenro Society Records may be found in Northeast Minnesota Historical Center, Duluth.

66. Theodore Jorgenson and Nora O. Solum, *Ole Edvart Rölvaag: A Biography*, 18, 26, 54–58 (New York, 1939). Here and below, see David Riesman, *Thorstein Veblen: A Critical Interpretation*, 206 (New York, 1953); Joseph Dorfman, *Thorstein Veblen and His America*, 3–13, 174, 504 (New York, 1934); George M. Frederickson, "Thorstein Veblen: The Last Viking," in *American Quarterly*, 11:403–15 (Fall 1959); Carlton C. Qualey, "Thorstein Bunde Veblen, 1857–1929," in Odd S. Lovoll, ed., *Makers of an American Immigrant Legacy: Essays in Honor of Kenneth O. Bjork*, 50–61 (Northfield, 1980).

67. Here and below, see Jorgenson and Solum, *Rölvaag*, 46–55, 155–59, 293–97, 340, 371.

68. Marion J. Nelson, "Herbjørn Gausta, Norwegian-American Painter," in Naess and Skard, eds., *Americana Norvegica*, 3:105–28; O. N. Nelson, comp., *History of the Scandinavians and Successful Scandinavians in the United States*, 1:404 (Minneapolis, 1893); Rena N. Coen, *Painting*

and *Sculpture in Minnesota, 1820–1914,* 71–74, 92 (Minneapolis, 1976); Marion J. Nelson, *Painting by Minnesotans of Norwegian Background, 1870–1970,* 34–36, 75 (Northfield, 2000); Marion J. Nelson, "Minnesota Painters of Norwegian Background, 1870–1970," in *Minnesota History,* 57:74–85 (Summer 2000); Hansen, *My Minneapolis,* 169–73; Luth Jaeger, "Two American Sculptors: Fjelde—Father and Son," in *American-Scandinavian Review,* 10:467–72 (August 1922).

69. Leola N. Bergmann, *Music Master of the Middle West: The Story of F. Melius Christiansen and the St. Olaf Choir,* 5, 21, 84. 114, 117, 131, 169, 195 (Minneapolis, 1944).

70. Marion Nelson, *Norwegian Folk Art: The Migration of a Tradition* (New York, 1995); Marion J. Nelson, ed., *Material Culture and People's Art among Norwegians in America* (Northfield, 1994); Philip Nusbaum, *Norwegian-American Music from Minnesota: Old-Time and Traditional Favorites,* 3–4 (St. Paul, 1989).

71. Nelson, *Norwegian Folk Art,* 95–97; Nusbaum, *Norwegian-American Music from Minnesota,* 4–12.

72. Gjerde, *Minds of the West,* 59–66; Orm Øverland, *Immigrant Minds, American Identities: Making the United States Home, 1870–1930,* 144–73 (Urbana, 2000); April R. Schultz, *Ethnicity on Parade: Inventing the Norwegian American through Celebration* (Amherst, Mass., 1994); Haugen, *Norwegian Language in America,* 1:240. For two of the standard works on the problem of assimilating or "Americanizing," see Milton M. Gordon, *Assimilation in American Life: The Role of Race, Religion, and National Origins* (New York, 1964); Joshua A. Fishman *et al., Language Loyalty in the United States* (The Hague, 1966).

73. Lovoll, *A Folk Epic,* 120; Carl H. Chrislock, "Introduction: The Historical Context," in Odd S. Lovoll, ed., *Cultural Pluralism* versus *Assimilation: The Views of Waldemar Ager,* 5 (Northfield, 1977).

74. Here and two paragraphs below, see Chrislock, "Introduction," and Kenneth Smemo, "Waldemar Theodore Ager," both in Lovoll, ed., *Cultural Pluralism,* 10–12, 16–18, 131; Einar Haugen, "The Struggle over Norwegian," in *Norwegian-American Studies,* 17:18, 19, 28 (Northfield, 1952); Skårdal, *Divided Heart,* 317–25. The Norwegian Society of America persisted until 1977; its publication, *Kvartalskrift,* ran from 1905 to 1922; Lovoll, ed., *Cultural Pluralism,* [i].

75. Theodore C. Blegen, *Minnesota: A History of the State,* 470–73 (Minneapolis, 1963). For more on the Public Safety Commission, see Carl H. Chrislock, *Watchdog of Loyalty: The Minnesota Commission of Public Safety during World War I* (St. Paul, 1991).

76. "D.J.G." reports, June 18, 20, 21, 1917, in Correspondence and Miscellaneous Records, Woman's Committee, Council of National Defense, War Records Commission Records, Minnesota State Archives, MHS; "The Scandinavian Press Service," appended to Nicolay A. Grevstad to A. C. Weiss, Oct. 30, 1917, File 117, and O. Morgan Norlie, "The Norwegian Parochial Schools," appended to Grevstad to C. W. Ames, Nov. 26, 1917, File 68, both in Minnesota Commission of Public Safety Records, State Archives. See also Carl H. Chrislock, *Ethnicity Challenged: The Upper Midwest Norwegian-American Experience in World War I* (Northfield, 1981).

77. Here and below, see Haugen, in *Norwegian-American Studies,* 17:29–31; Lovoll, *A Folk Epic,* 138; Chrislock, in Lo-

voll, ed., *Cultural Pluralism*, 34; Andersen, *Norwegian-Americans*, 193.

78. Jorgenson and Solum, *Rölvaag*, 293–95; Haugen, in *Norwegian-American Studies*, 17:32–34; Ole E Rølvaag, *Concerning Our Heritage*, trans. and ed. Solveig Zempel (Northfield, 1998) is a translation of *Omkring Fædrearven* published in 1922.

79. Haugen, *Norwegian Language in America*, 1:263, 264; Haugen, in *Norwegian-American Studies*, 17:5; Dorothy C. A. Pederson, "Pope County Area Lutheran Churches Shift from Norwegian to English," 20, term paper, University of Minnesota, Morris, 1976, copy in West Central Minnesota Historical Research Center, Morris; Peter A. Munch, "The Church as Complementary Identity," in Erik J. Friis, ed., *The Scandinavian Presence in North America*, 64 (New York, 1976).

80. Øverland, *Immigrant Minds, American Identities*, 144–73; Schultz, *Ethnicity on Parade;* Lovoll, *A Folk Epic*, 164–71; Lovoll and Bjork, *Norwegian-American Historical Association*, 15; Haugen, in *Norwegian-American Studies*, 17:34. Inspired by the centennial of organized Norwegian immigration to the U.S., a filiopietistic work on Norwegian-American women, Alma A. Guttersen and Regina Hilleboe Christensen, eds., *Norse-American Women, 1825–1925* (St. Paul, 1926), reflected the attitudes of the elite women who wrote the articles in it as well as the general tone of ethnic celebratory volumes of that day. The Immigration Act of 1924 allotted an annual quota of 2,377 to Norway.

81. Lovoll and Bjork, *Norwegian-American Historical Association*, 30–32; Norborg, *American Saga*, 141–44, 161, 191; A. N. Rygg, *American Relief for Norway*, 8 (Chicago, 1947); Andersen, *Norwegian-*Americans, 202; Haugen, *Norwegian Language in America*, 1:275, 277; Hansen, *History of Sons of Norway*, 371.

82. Rygg, *American Relief for Norway*, 208–221. Many of the organizations were still functioning in 1980, including the Progressive Literary Club, "a group of women united to pursue mutual interests in their Norse heritage and to study the contributions of that nation to our culture," which dated from 1921; copy of organizational literature in MEHP Papers.

83. Here and two paragraphs below, see Odd S. Lovoll, "From Norway to America: A Tradition of Immigration Fades," in Dennis L. Cuddy, ed., *Contemporary American Immigration: Interpretive Essays* (Boston, 1982); United States Scandinavian statistics in MEHP Papers, compiled by Jon A. Gjerde from U.S. Justice Dept., Immigration and Naturalization Service reports for those years (Minnesota figures are not available because Norwegians were counted with Danes and Swedes); 90 Congress, 1 session, House of Representatives, Committee on Government Operations, *The Brain Drain into the United States of Scientists, Engineers, and Physicians: A Staff Study*, 18, 28, 30, 40, 42, 52, 54, 64, 76, 78, 88 (Washington, D.C., 1967); Kenneth Bjork, *Saga in Steel and Concrete: Norwegian Engineers in America* (Northfield, 1947); Hugh Carter, "Social Characteristics of Naturalized Americans from Norway," in Immigration and Naturalization Service, *Monthly Review*, 9:59 (November 1951). On the Leif Erikson statue, see *St. Paul Pioneer Press*, Oct. 10, 1949, p. 1.

84. Lovoll and Bjork, *Norwegian-American Historical Association*, 5–8.

85. *Minneapolis Tribune*, May 4, 1980, p. 16F; *Star Tribune*, June 17, 2001, p. 1B, 9B.

86. Kathleen Stokker, *Keeping Christmas: Yuletide Traditions in Norway and the New Land* (St. Paul, 2000).

87. On *Mindekirken,* see *Minneapolis Tribune,* March 22, 1980, p. 1B; mindekirken.org. Among a sample of Lutheran churches of Norwegian background in Iowa in 1972, pastors under the age of 50 were found to be using the Norwegian language in services more and more, and 90% reported growing interest in ethnic backgrounds on the part of their parishioners; see Duane R. Lindberg, "Ethnic Awareness Among Clergy and Parishioners," in Friis, ed., *Scandinavian Presence,* 70–76. On the Sons of Norway, see Harry Johnson to Jon Gjerde, Sept. 24, 1979, in MEHP Papers; membership numbers from Sons of Norway office, Minneapolis. *Rosemaling* is the decorative art of flower painting as interior decoration or on wooden objects. The sword that inspired the Ulen festival was discussed in *The Forum* (Fargo-Moorhead), Oct. 22, 1979, p. 1. A telling comment on the self-image some Twin Cities Norwegian Americans cultivated in the 1970s was the effort—an unsuccessful one—by Norwegian groups to move the statue of violinist Ole Bull from Loring Park, which they considered disreputable, to a close association with Minnesota's cultural elite on the Peavey Plaza next to Minneapolis' Orchestra Hall; *Minneapolis Tribune,* Sept. 7, 1978, p. 9B.

88. Jorgenson and Solum, *Rölvaag,* 295.

Index

Page numbers in italic refer to pictures and captions.

Minnesota Commission of Public Safety, 61

Moe, Roger, 47

Moland, 19

Mondale, Walter, 47

Mower County, 8

Music, 27, 53–56; bands, *23, 55;* choral, 53–54; folk, 54–56

Muskego, Wisc., 4–5; church, *5,* 89*n*46

Muus, Bernt J., 37

Nelson, Knute, 41, 45

Newspapers, account of agricultural success, 21–22; encourage immigration, 16–17, 39–40, 77–80; as literature, 49; Norwegian language, 38, 61–63; politics in, 41, 61–62; publishing and writing as occupation, 27

Nilsson, Christina, 31

Noah's Ark (Beard's Block), *27,* 28

Norman County, 20; ladies aid, *35;* wheat harvest, *21*

Norwegian-American Historical Association, 64–65

Norwegian Lutheran Memorial Church, *75*

Occupations and employment, banking, 20; fishing industry, 23–24; lumber industry, 23; options in Norway, 2; professions, 27–28, 68–69; publishing and writing, 27, 31, 32; of women, 28

Olds, Ben, *44*

Olmsted County, 8

Olson, Anna and Martin, *21*

Olson, Floyd B., 41, 46, *46*

Oral histories, 86*n*20, 87*n*29

Organizations, identity and involvement, 59–60; pan-Scandinavian secular, 30–31; wartime, 67, 93*n*82

Parades, *58,* 59, *59,* 73

Park Region settlements, 14, *14*

Pennington County, 20

Politics, agriculture and, 43–45; controversies, 34–35; newspapers and, 41; pan-Scandinavian, 41, 43; Republican Party, 42–44; Sioux Agency politicians, *44;* socioeconomics and, 47; third party, 41–42, 43–46; urban, 45; Viking Leagues, 43–44; women in, *48*

Polk County, 19–20

Population, immigration, 1–2; in Norway, 2–3; second-generation, 69–70; statistics, 83*n*2; in Twin Cities, 26–27, 29–30. *See also* Settlement patterns

Prejudice, against Catholics, 46; wartime hysteria, 20–21

Quie, Al, 47

Railroads, 20; station, *25*

Ramsey County, 29–30

Red Lake County, 20

Red River Valley, 14, 18–21, 78–79

Red Wing Seminary, *37,* 38

Regional groups, Hallings, 9–11, 16, 17, *33;* socioeconomics and, 17; Stavangers, 8; Telemarks, 16; Tronders, 17

Rekkedahl, Ragna, *22*

Religion, religious freedom, 35–36; religious prejudice, 46. *See also* individual denominations

Remigrants, 25–26, 68

Republican Party, 42–44, 47

Restauration, model of, 2

Rice, Ole A., 21

Rice County, 8

Roseau County, 20–21

Rølvaag, Ole E., 49–52, *51,* 57, 63, 76

Rosendahl, Peter, cartoons by, *33, 40*

Rosendahl family, *10*

Rural life, husmenn (cotters) in Norway, 2–3; as Norwegian ideal, 18, 21–23,

Picture Credits

Names of the photographers, when known, are in parentheses following the page number on which the picture appears.

Minnesota Historical Society—page x, 2 (K. L. Fenney), 5 (Eugene D. Becker), 12 (Ole Aarseth), 15, 16 (John Johnson), 17 (*St. Paul Dispatch and Pioneer Press*), 22 (Ole Aarseth), 24, 25 (Gilbert B. Ellestad), 26, 27, 29, 31, 35, 37 (Edward H. Lidberg), 42 (Edmonston), 44 (Ole Aarseth), 46, 48, 50 (Underwood and Underwood), 51, 53 (*Minneapolis Star-Journal*), 54 (bottom; Monroe P. Killy), 55, 56, 58, 59 (Skage Brothers), 65 (K. L. Fenney), 67, 68, 69, 71 (*St. Paul Dispatch and Pioneer Press*), 72

Private collection—page 10 (Peter Rosendahl), 11 (Chris Engell and Son), 23 (Chris Engell and Son), 33 (Peter Rosendahl), 40 (Peter Rosendahl)

Otter Tail County Historical Society, Fergus Falls—page 14 (W. T. Oxley)

Eva Hedstrom—page 19

Norman County Historical Society, Ada—page 21

Vesterheim Norwegian-American Museum, Decorah, Iowa—page 52

Minneapolis Star Tribune—page 54 (top; Wally Kammenn)

Mindekirken, Norwegian Lutheran Memorial Church, Minneapolis—page 75 (both)

Acknowledgments

Grateful thanks are due to Georgia Rosendahl and Chad Muller from Spring Grove, Edna Rude of Gary (Norman County), and Kaia Knutson from Mindekirken in Minneapolis.

Minnesotans can trace their families and their state's heritage to a multitude of ethnic groups. *The People of Minnesota* series tells each group's story in a compact, handsomely illustrated, and accessible paperback. Readers will learn about the group's accomplishments, ethnic organizations, settlement patterns, and occupations. Each book includes a personal story of one person or family, told through a diary, a letter, or an oral history.

In his introduction to the series, Bill Holm reminds us why these stories are as important as ever: "To be ethnic, somehow, is to be human. Neither can we escape it, nor should we want to. You cannot interest yourself in the lives of your neighbors if you don't take sufficient interest in your own."

This series is based on the critically acclaimed book *They Chose Minnesota: A Survey of the State's Ethnic Groups* (Minnesota Historical Society Press). The volumes in *The People of Minnesota* bring each group's story up to date and add dozens of photographs to inform and enhance the telling.

Books in the series include *Irish in Minnesota, Jews in Minnesota, Norwegians in Minnesota,* and *African Americans in Minnesota.*

Bill Holm is the grandson of four Icelandic immigrants to Minneota, Minnesota, where he still lives. He is the author of eight books including *Eccentric Island: Travels Real and Imaginary* and *Coming Home Crazy.* When he is not practicing the piano or on the road circuit-riding for literature, he teaches at Southwest State University in Marshall, Minnesota.

About the Authors

Jon Gjerde is professor of history at University of California, Berkeley, and author of *The Minds of the West: Ethnocultural Evolution in the Rural Middle West, 1830–1917.*

Carlton C. Qualey was a professor at Carleton College, editor of *Immigration History Newsletter,* and author of *Norwegian Settlement in the United States.*